CANBERRA

Paul Daley is a Sydney-based author, essayist and multi-award-winning journalist who writes about history, Australian national identity and Indigenous culture in his column 'Postcolonial' for *The Guardian*. Author of *On Patriotism* and the political thriller *Challenge*, his forthcoming novel, *Jesustown* will be out in 2021.

YASS
(59 km)

NEW SOUTH WALES
AUSTRALIAN CAPITAL TERRITORY

LAKE
GINNINDERRA

Arboretum

MOLONGLO
RIVER

Mount
Stromlo

Albert Hall

MURRUMBIDGEE RIVER

BRINDABELLA
RANGES

COTTER
RIVER

TUGGERANONG

GUNDAROO
(38 km)
LAKE
GEORGE
GUNGAHLIN
Black
Mountain
Tower
Black
Mountain
Mount
Ainslie
Australian War Memorial
ACTON
REID
Australian War Memorial
LAKE
BURLEY
GRIFFIN
CIVIC
Anzac Parade
Constitution Avenue
DUNTROON
Albert Hall
National Library of Australia
Parliament
House
Telopea
Park
PIALLIGO
KINGSTON
MANUKA
National Library of Australia
FYSHWICK
Parliament House
WODEN
RED HILL
O'MALLEY
QUEANBEYAN

Other titles in the City Series
Hobart by Peter Timms, with a foreword by Robert Dessaix
Brisbane by Matthew Condon
Sydney by Delia Falconer
Melbourne by Sophie Cunningham
Adelaide by Kerryn Goldsworthy
Perth by David Whish-Wilson
Darwin by Tess Lea

'*Canberra* is both a history and a personal love story'
– *The Saturday Age*

'(Daley's) narration of the history of the place, and of the city erected on it, is done with flair and aplomb, making *Canberra* among other things the best concise, broad-brush Canberra history yet. It would be good if all of Canberra turned into one big book club and read *Canberra*, so as to be able to natter about it, be stimulated by it and fight duels over it. The book is unique. Because Canberra is such a young city, it has never had a soliloquy like this written about it before.' – Ian Warden, *The Canberra Times*

'... Daley has unveiled a side of the city that many do not see.' – *The Adelaide Advertiser*

'Daley is at his best when writing about his own life in, and in relation to, Canberra. The scenes that depict him walking his dog through Red Hill, or looking out across the limestone plains, evoke the environment richly, sensually. In these passages, and those that locate his family in the story of the town, he achieves presence, image, and a quality of writing that brings Canberra sharply into focus ... I found that *Canberra* offers many exquisite moments. – *Australian Book Review*

'Paul Daley's *Canberra* ... begins with the strong Indigenous history of Canberra, and moves forward through its pastoral iteration and on to the great nation-building project that is Canberra's reason for existence. There are many twists and turns along the way, particularly as the grand idea of Canberra is often let down by the realities of narrow-minded pragmatism or political ambition. However, Daley is aware that Canberra is actually a place where people live, and it is in these "local" moments that the book is revealing and enticing. This book presents an opportunity to re-engage with the ideas behind, and the history of, our nation's capital city.' – *BOOKSELLER+PUBLISHER*

'Paul Daley has unveiled a side of the city that many do not see. He talks about its rich history from its first use as a huge grazing property and how it became the nation's capital. It is not an easy thing to pull off, getting people to like Canberra. There's no in-between – you either love it or hate it. Where Daley succeeds is in making Canberra appear to be a much more interesting place to live in than many people believe to be the case.' – *The Adelaide Advertiser*

CANBERRA

PAUL
DALEY

For Lenore Taylor – the reason I stayed

A NewSouth book

Published by
NewSouth Publishing
University of New South Wales Press Ltd
University of New South Wales
Sydney NSW 2052
AUSTRALIA
newsouthpublishing.com

First published 2012
New edition 2020

10 9 8 7 6 5 4 3 2 1

A catalogue record for this book is available from the National Library of Australia

ISBN: 9781742237046 (paperback)
9781742244952 (ebook)
9781742249490 (ePDF)

Cover design Sandy Cull, gogoGingko
Internal design Josephine Pajor-Markus
Cover photo gettyimages / Peter Guo
Map David Atkinson, handmademaps.com
Printer Griffin Press

Contents

For here have we no continuing city

But seek one to come

Hebrews 13:14

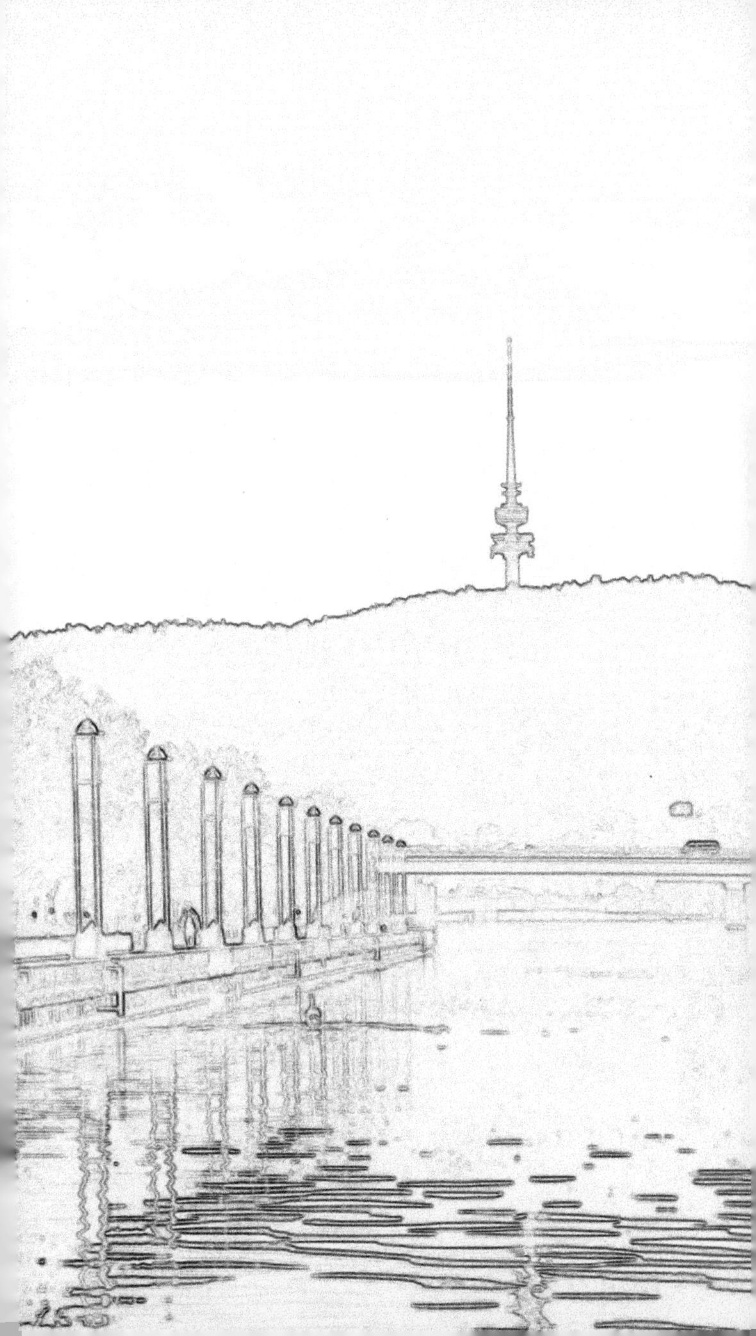

Prologue

My father lifted me with straining arms. I was eye-to-nose with that man who was so familiar to me from the television. But he looked past me to the base of the steps below where a big white car waited, its front passenger door open and a chauffeur beside it. Expert in the unteachable political skill of non-engaged engagement, he was undoubtedly dealing with us. But his attention was focused ten steps beyond; he gestured theatrically with those dark eyebrows, to the driver.

'Paul,' my father Patrick said, although he was actually addressing the great man, 'this is the next Prime Minister of Australia.'

'Correct, comrade,' he said. 'I am.'

'Shake hands,' Dad said, again addressing – ordering – Edward Gough Whitlam. He extended his hand.

I watched from below as Dad, who had swiftly deposited me onto the ground, used both hands to envelop and vigorously pump that which he viewed no less reverently than God's. When Dad released Whitlam, my sister, five years older and a good deal taller than me, shook his hand too. I didn't get the chance.

Then he bounced in great strides, a gazelle in grey flannel, down Parliament's steps and into the car. Dad watched admiringly as Whitlam's car disappeared into the mist.

Early memories become fickle with age. It's not always possible to inflame the flickering embers of recollection that smoulder around distant childhood experiences.

But that chance meeting with Whitlam outside the provisional Parliament House during a family driving holiday from Melbourne to Canberra in early 1970 has always been much more than a mere smudge on my consciousness.

It is a defining childhood memory.

Today, when I stand on the steps of Old Parliament House, with its sculpted vista of undulating lawn, of lake, of low mountains, of Aboriginal Tent Embassy and war memorial, with that earthy mildew scent of cold stone, I'm back four decades ago with Whitlam.

I remember being irritated at not having shaken

Whitlam's hand; that was, so I'd thought, the aim. But I was only six and incapable of fully processing what had passed between he and my father.

I recall, however, being unsettled by the sight of my solid, reliable father – modest, and always suspicious of fame and egotism – become a fawning, less certain *somebody else* in the glowing Whitlam aura. A discomforting unease visits me whenever that beautiful old building triggers the dormant memory.

But something else happened. It would take decades for me to divine the emotional place of that day in my parents' marriage.

Now I mostly understand.

Dad, an ALP man whose father served as a Labor councillor in 1930s Melbourne, was among the legion of fans under Whitlam's spell as the times propelled Gough to the prime ministership.

Mum, I recall, stood remote from the small group that surrounded Whitlam. She was small, ivory-skinned and raven-haired, strikingly beautiful in middle age. She reserved her intimidating dark-Irish stare for the most egregious offenders against the political, social and religious sensibilities that guided her. And so she glowered her daggers from the wings at the spectacle – at her entranced husband who'd abruptly dropped her son so he might clutch Whitlam, and then at her daughter shaking *his* hand.

Mum would have looked forward to that trip to Canberra. She had probably not been there since about 1955. Back when Robert Menzies was still tracking to become Australia's longest-serving prime minister. And back when Herbert Vere Evatt was making his mark as the most brilliant but flawed leader in opposition of a Labor Party that he was tearing apart. Our mother's memories of Canberra were vivid and mostly fond.

In later life she spoke of the Menzies charm and presence and of the avuncular Ben Chifley, who would bounce her brother Bill's daughter on his knee behind his desk.

As we walked to the car at Old Parliament House that day in 1970, Mum and Dad bickered about Whitlam, while Dad told us how, when the 'stuttering idiot' Duke of York opened Parliament House in 1927, nobody had turned up and all the uneaten pies were buried at the spot where an administration building later grew. The public service, Dad said, was definitely built on meat pies. I believed him, of course.

As we drove away, Dad raised his voice at Mum.

I remember, because he did this so rarely.

What he said didn't make sense to me.

But I knew what I thought.

I hated Whitlam.

I hated politics.

And I hated Canberra.

I wanted never to come back.

Twenty-three years later I was moving in.

Three sinewy men in black footy shorts, singlets and Blundstones unloaded from a truck what few possessions I hadn't either given away or sold in my haste to leave Melbourne. The truck was parked half on the clipped verge of a narrow crescent, canopied by mature exotic oaks in full, luscious foliage. We were out front of a block of copybook-neat apartments in Kingston, a suburb in Canberra's inner south that I had been assured (wrongly) was 'lively' enough to provide me with the inner-city Melbourne trappings to which I was accustomed.

I'd been to Canberra but once since that 1970 holiday, on a school trip when I was sixteen. We stayed at an Australian National University college. We absconded at night and got drunk at a dive in

Civic. We went to the Australian War Memorial, the National Gallery and the old Anatomy School. We picnicked by the lake. We went to Parliament House, where I relived my parents' fight.

Although pleasant, the visit didn't assuage my prejudices or uncomfortable memories. Politics both repelled and fascinated me. Like most Australians, politics was for me synonymous with Canberra.

But here I was, moving to the city I'd sworn off as a six-year-old.

The Kingston apartment block, with its angular façade, that was about to become my home, resembled the few that had been left standing in Sarajevo, a city I'd only recently passed through while writing about the latest Balkans war. I was twenty-nine, with shared custody of a little girl. I had just ended yet another relationship. I was in a deep funk, possibly – I realise now – due to my experiences in Bosnia. I was ready to walk away from a promising journalism career when I surprised myself by agreeing with my editor that I should move to Canberra to cover politics.

'Besides,' he'd assured me, 'there's heaps of single women there – you'll get loads of sex.'

I had resisted other entreaties to Canberra for work. This was the most compelling professional proposition that I'd had in a while, even though I actually wanted nothing more than to be truly alone. I wanted isolation and I wanted anonymity. London, Berlin and Washington weren't options.

Today, I am bemused at my naivety at expecting to find solitude or anonymity here.

In Canberra, a physically isolated city of secrets, everyone knows – or at least wants to know – your business.

'Excuse me gentlemen, but you can't park your lorry there,' said a man of a certain age who, I would later appreciate, wore the standard garb of the retired Canberra public servant of that era: pastel polo shirt, pressed fawn slacks and loafers. 'It's a public space and besides, the wheels will ruin the lawn.'

Fawn Slacks was doing nothing to provide an auspicious start to my new beginning.

I was already an apostle of the cliché that this was an unfeeling, fabricated faux 'city' – a country town with a hyper-inflated sense of being that was peopled by constipated bureaucrats who obsequiously served politicians who themselves couldn't stand the place. To my mind Canberra was poisoned by politics. It was not *of* real Australia but existed to do things to it.

My family had already been well and truly Canberra-ed.

I was ready to tell the boys to take my stuff home to Melbourne.

That evening I went to the local supermarket. John Gorton, Australia's nineteenth prime minister, stood at the cash register before me, purchasing a flagon of cream sherry. He shuffled out on his walking stick and got into a Commonwealth car.

Hmm. Might be interesting after all, I thought.

Some people who live in Canberra genuinely don't worry about what anyone thinks of their city. And then there are those who say they don't care because Canberra is 'a hidden gem' – 'Australia's best kept secret' – and 'we don't want everyone coming here, do we?'

But when you've lived here for a while it's obvious that those who really don't care are few.

Canberrans are notoriously satisfied with their lot. They also have a great sense of entitlement. With their big houses, first-class schools, their pristine blue-skied winters and hot dry summers, with their garden suburbs separated by bush corridors in a natural mountainous amphitheatre, with their proximity to some of the continent's best beaches and skifields, with their beautiful multi-lane traffic-free roads and bike paths, and with their abundant fine restaurants and sporting facilities, why wouldn't they be?

It's surprising, then, that they should be simultaneously so conspicuously self-conscious, hyper-defensive and incredulous that Canberra isn't Australia's envy.

This is not the type of proud parochialism that has defined the 'mine is bigger than yours' grudge contest between Melbourne and Sydney since early colonial days.

No, it's a tetchy defensiveness bordering on paranoia that is firmly rooted in Australia's underlying contempt for Canberra, a place that has been vilified and misunderstood since it was named a century ago.

Anyone who drives more than a hundred kilometres from Canberra with Australian Capital Territory number plates will get a sense of how it feels to be Canberran.

'Given yourself a pay-rise too?' a bloke at the next pump at a petrol station in rural Victoria demanded of me last summer, referring to a Remuneration

Tribunal ruling that had just awarded federal politicians more money.

Should I begin, I wondered, with an explanation of proportional representation in the House of Representatives or the Senate quota system?

I reverted to a well-rehearsed stock answer: 'Mate, there's 226 MPs in federal Parliament and only four come from Canberra.'

'Doesn't matter,' he said, 'you're all bloody public servants so it comes back to you in the end.'

Such boof-headed ignorance relies on a premise that bureaucracy is intrinsically useless because it is not profit-driven, and that there is no nobility in dedicating one's life to public service through the pursuit of civil society, scientific and environmental research, justice, defence, the arts or foreign service.

I understand why so many residents find it deeply offensive and hurtful; the underlying viscerally held national sentiment is that not only is their city unworthy, but so, too, are its people.

It's nothing new. Australia has been belting Canberra since the city's foundation in 1913. No end of patient explanation or inclusive celebration of the centenary will destigmatise the place in a hurry.

Canberra has no real option but to get over itself – to stop worrying about what everyone else thinks. Easily said.

Some things about Canberra irritate – even infuriate – me. Not least its social claustrophobia, its veneer of smug self-satisfaction, its self-absorbed NIMBY-ness and its pervasive self-defeating defensiveness.

Nonetheless, after living here for twenty years I get angry when outsiders revert to the old clichés when criticising the city as a soulless place of endless roundabouts and meaningless public monuments, of sub-standard restaurants – a 'lights-out' place populated solely by drone-like bureaucrats and politicians. That these criticisms are made by people who've rarely been here, learnt the city's story or its *raison d'être* annoys me more because Canberra, as the national capital, is every Australian's city.

'But it's boring,' some of my friends say, condescendingly. 'Nothing ever happens in Canberra – and its history is *so* dull.'

I'm tempted to tell them about the hunter-gathering Aboriginal tribes that wandered the great plains upon which the city was built, about the tough-as-nails pioneers and Waterloo veterans who stole their land, whose convicts went wild and who then fought the bushrangers, and about the bushfires and the floods. I don't tell them about the stoic settler women, about the adventure of federation that led to a great battle of the potential capital sites, or about the World War I veterans, the sounds of shellfire still ringing in their heads, who constructed their capital.

I don't tell them because first they would have to understand Canberra is the manifestation of a dream – an ideal that a beautiful, well-planned and purpose-built city could represent the best of what Australian federation could aspire to. Canberra, it was envisaged, would be a display home for the country's anthropology and culture and learning, as well as its decision-makers. It would be Australia's objective historical memory and its conscience, its vanguard of scientific research and the showcase for its creativity. It would be a national monument to those who'd died in its conflicts and a repository of the archives, every Australian paper and book, the art and artefacts that signposted our complex and morally fraught road through nationhood.

Canberra was supposed to symbolise the new Australian democracy.

But politics compromised it from inception.

Despite all the hurdles that Canberra has faced, its evolution comes – ironically and almost by accident – so very close to embodying the dreamers' dreams, and as a triumph of hope and enlightenment over cynicism.

Canberra is an accidental miracle.

The Plains

In the beginning the plains were a vast expanse of limestone. Then the native groundcovers transformed them into one great blanket of colour as the button daisies, bluebells and vivid yellow kangaroo grass took root in brittle, rich soil.

The eucalypt, melaleuca, casuarina and grevillea stuck to the edges of the rises and gathered in occasional thicker copses around the rolling hills bordering the plains. It was a perfect natural grassland furrowed with a series of bubbling streams and faster-flowing, darker brooks that connected a series of billabongs. The Ngambri were the first inhabitants.

The Ngambri people wielded spears and boomerangs to take the emu and bustard, the kangaroo, wallaby and wallaroo, the bream and freshwater crayfish. They also needed weapons to fight off the others who trespassed to hunt and to steal their women. They were people such as the Ngurmal who shared the same Walgalu language group, the Woradgery, and yet others from the north like the Wallabalooa and Cookmai who spoke Ngunnawal.

It was Ngambri land originally. But others came, seeking permission to cross the rivers and in times of abundance to hunt the birds and animals and the fatty bogong moths that swarmed each spring.

'All around there, including around the Molonglo was grassland. It was perfect, beautifully managed grassland. If you can imagine it, it was so alive with food that the women would dig for yam daisies to go with the meat that the men hunted,' Ngambri elder Shane Mortimer explained to me.

This place could only have seemed like a woman: the two mountains to the north were her breasts, the basin – with its marsupials and moths, its birds and fish – was her fertile womb, and the wide expanse of snow-capped ranges to the south, her hips.

The argument about how Canberra, the city that would defiantly grow out of the plains, earned its name will never be settled to everyone's satisfaction. But some insist, with good reason, that it is a derivative of the word 'Ngambri', variously written by whites as Canbery, Canberry or even Kamberri or Kemberri, which might just mean a 'woman's breasts'.

Others maintain it means 'meeting place', for that's what the plains were for the Ngambri who lived there and the many other peoples who passed by.

Most days I wander about Red Hill, a steep escarpment of protected native bush that stands behind my house. I go there to muse among the trees, to run through the elements with my dog, a black girl Labrador who snuffles tentatively at the crevices beneath the volcanic boulders and around the great fallen trees that have been smoothed away, as if by sandpaper, by decades of sleet and breeze. The potent scent of the 'roos, blue-tongues, snakes and foxes arouses her twitchy senses. She chases the big eastern greys when they bounce into her pitifully short visual periphery. She'll race off after them, possessed, on the strength of the flimsiest whiff or a telling papery crunch. They'd tear her open with their sharp claws if ever she caught up. But she never does – and she wouldn't know what to do if she did. I sometimes think that even the dogs of Canberra are self-satisfied; in most other big Australian cities they must content themselves with ball and stick.

If I look north across the plains from here, it's easy to appreciate a décolletage, more gentle than buxom, between the mountains – Black and Ainslie.

Because I know what to look for I can also discern the ghostly outline of a century-old cityscape – a utopia that would only ever find completion in Marion Mahony Griffin's breathtakingly beautiful pictures. Marion articulated the dream of her landscape architect husband, Walter Griffin, using a three-stage process that ended with watercolour and photographic dye images on roller-blind fabric.

Wooed by Marion's art, Australia chose the plan that Griffin somehow conjured in his office overlooking Lake Michigan in Chicago over a period of just nine weeks. And then Australia mostly ignored the plan, abandoning the drawings along with the Griffins.

The land axis stretches out below me – an invisible line running from Parliament House and across the lake to the Australian War Memorial. This axis dissects a great inverted 'V' that also begins at Parliament House. One of its triangular lines ends at an awkward place called City Hill that today stands isolated in the middle of a monolithic traffic roundabout. The other finishes at Russell Hill, the home of Australia's military leaders, who ignore and scoff at their political masters across a lake that, ironically, takes the name 'Burley Griffin' from a man Canberra's ultimate planners so obstinately shunned.

A notional intersecting water axis cuts south-east to north-west across the Griffins' lake. The bones of the Griffin plan are subtly though defiantly evident from up here on Red Hill, like the veins of a leaf when held to the light. Within and around the triangle you can still find elements of the faded geometric Griffin blueprint – in the wide boulevards, the hexagons and circles that have been filled in – with the more prosaic plans of others, with public monuments and buildings (along with suburbs in the name of prime ministers and early settlers) whose symbolism is largely lost on the country to which they were dedicated. And filled too, of course, with many of the millions of trees that constitute Canberra's stunning urban forest. The Ngambri's grasslands were long ago planted with an array of exotic and colourful flora as part of its 'reforestation'. It's true this land was ruined by the white man's hoofed animals and even more so by his plague rabbits. Planting all those trees made it look better. As becoming as the urban forest below me looks today, these plains were never – as so many white men insist – previously covered in trees.

Given Mahony Griffin's under-valued contribution, it seems appropriate that Canberra was thought of as woman from the Dreamtime.

One of the plains' pioneers, John Gale, who arrived in 1855, was taken with such symbolism.

In his *Canberra History and Legends,* published in 1927, he writes, 'It not only struck me as being supremely poetic, but also singularly appropriate to the site chosen as the mother city of the Australian Commonwealth.'

Initially I reckon this is probably just another yarn told by white men in the Queanbeyan pubs.

It's like so much of what Gale wrote and said. It's hard to be certain what to believe.

He came here barely three decades after the first whites arrived with their sheep. As he wrote about Canberra towards the very end of his life in 1927, Gale was being hailed as the longest continuously working and the oldest professional writer in the English language. Many consider Gale to be the founding father of Canberra, so energetically did he push for the Australian capital to be built on the plains – despite living in Queanbeyan, the New South Wales town still engaged in a lively provincial supremacy argument with its neighbour.

By the time Gale got here, the Limestone Plains had already become a vast dusty paddock. The area was divided into a series of stock stations belonging to a few wealthy squatters, later to become free-holders – if they were fortunate enough to receive such valuable grants courtesy of the New South Wales administration. The white man's arrival on the plains was an inevitable result of the south-westerly push through of animals and stock tracks by explorers who were commissioned to expand the colony at Port Jackson.

Today, the men at the vanguard would be described as an eclectic, even 'colourful', bunch. Among them were hardened veterans of the French Revolutionary and Napoleonic Wars, ticket-of-leave convicts, a renowned ship's surgeon. There was also a colonial trader, Robert Campbell, a principal ally of the deposed New South Wales governor, Vice Admiral William Bligh, and a contemporary and admirer of the enlightened British MP and anti-slavery activist, William Wilberforce.

'Merchant Campbell', as he was known, came from a wealthy trading family whose company, Campbell & Co., imported goods to England from Calcutta. From 1798, Campbell used his family's ships to build a lucrative trading connection between India and Port Jackson. After buying land just inside Dawes Point (close to The Rocks), Campbell built a private wharf and warehouses to accommodate his thriving business.

Sydney, an expanding penitentiary, struggled to feed itself. Crops were subject to the fickleness of a harsh antipodean climate; livestock were few and expensive.

In March 1806 floods destroyed most of the colony's crops. Commandeering one of Campbell's ships, the *Sydney*, Governor Philip King ordered it to sail immediately for Calcutta and return with food for the starving colony.

Gale explained what happened in his book, in which he artfully weaves what seems to be quite often third- and even fourth-hand historical 'faction', with gruesome details of made-for-tabloid crimes, rumour and curious happenstance.

> Just then there arrived in Port Jackson a couple of ships on their way to England with full cargoes of valuable furs, the fruit of some years' seal hunting in the south seas. The then governor saw in the timely arrival of these ships a practical means of averting the threatening famine. The ships were

> seized, their valuable cargoes dumped out on to the sandy foreshores of Sydney Cove, and the ships' captains ordered to proceed to the Cape of Good Hope for the much needed breadstuffs. The vessels were never afterwards heard of, and as for the furs, they had altogether perished and become worthless.

Although Gale believed two ships were involved, other accounts say there was only one. The *Sydney* is said to have been wrecked off the coast of New Guinea.

It was probably Bligh – Campbell having served him loyally as the colony's treasurer – who agreed to compensation for the loss. But compensation didn't arrive until the early 1820s, when Campbell was granted 710 sheep and a swathe of prime grazing land on the colony's south-eastern frontier.

Campbell became the first owner-occupier on the Limestone Plains.

But he was not the first white man to venture there.

That honour belonged to ticket-of-leave convict Joseph Wild and his master Charles Throsby, a brilliant but melancholic ship's surgeon who served Britain at sea in the French Revolutionary Wars.

Dr Throsby arrived in Port Jackson aboard the *Coromandel* on 13 June 1802 after crossing from England, still as a ship's surgeon, with a load of about 140 convicts and a few dozen free settlers. Because all who boarded the *Coromandel* at the Thames survived the voyage to disembark in Sydney, Throsby won immediate acclaim from King, who promptly earmarked him as a reliable colonial servant.

By April 1805 Throsby was commander of the penal colony at Newcastle where 'he controlled the settlement with zeal and success until the year 1809, when he resigned on account of ill health', as Frederick Watson's 1927 *A Brief History of Canberra* puts it. Throsby settled on a 1500-acre pastoral expanse at Minto, where he ran cattle, granted in exchange for his services at Newcastle. But Throsby was restless. He and his workers pushed into the high country and then along the southern coastal plains; in 1816 he settled in the Illawarra district and built huts in Moss Vale. Then in 1818 he reached Jervis Bay.

From the Southern Highlands, Throsby made at least five expeditions – some on contract to the New South Wales government – to chart the 'New Country' further inland to the south and on the coast. He found much-needed grazing country around Bathurst and blazed a pass, through which to drive stock, from the Illawarra to Robertson in the highlands. In 1820 Governor Lachlan Macquarie commissioned Throsby to build a road from the Southern Highlands at Cowpastures, near Exeter, into the unexplored southern frontier around the Goulburn Plains. Throsby put his man Wild in charge of the convict road-building party.

Wild – also known as 'Wilde' – was transported from England to Australia for life in 1797 for burglary. By the time he won his ticket of leave in 1810, the illiterate Wild was one of the colony's most accomplished bushmen. Unlike many free men and ticket-of-leavers, Wild – like his master Throsby – made great efforts to understand the culture and languages of the Aboriginal peoples around Sydney who were being dispossessed by the race for new pastoral settlements.

While building the road, Throsby was told by Aboriginal people about a large lake – 'Wee-ree-naa'. About two days further on, they said, was a tidal river – 'Murrumbidgee' or 'Murrumbeeja'. Throsby sent Wild, described as being superbly fit in his early sixties, to find the lake. According to the Australian Bureau of Statistics 1931 *Official Year Book of the Commonwealth of Australia,* it was late August in 1820 when Wild and several others, possibly including two Aboriginal people, set off.

They quickly found the lake and followed its eastern shore. After camping on the banks for two nights they emerged at Turullo Creek, near today's town of Bungendore. On 22 August Wild left the other men and ascended a rise later known as Gibraltar Mountain. The horizon was dominated, as Wild told Throsby, by the 'Snowy Mountains to the SW'. Wild thus became the first white man to see the continent's highest ranges.

While camping that night Wild noticed the lake's level dropped by about six inches. He could have been forgiven for assuming that the lake was tidal. Visiting the newly discovered lake in late October 1820 Governor Macquarie named it 'George' after King George III. Wild, I assume, told the governor about the lake's oscillating level, a phenomenon that remains mysterious.

Meanwhile, Throsby, determined to find the Murrumbidgee, set off in search of the river while

Macquarie was still in camp. He didn't find it, instead heading back to Macquarie, Wild and the others after reaching the country around Gungahlin – what is today a satellite town on the northern extremity of the Australian Capital Territory.

Determined to find the elusive Murrumbidgee, Throsby dispatched Wild and two others, including Charles Throsby Smith – his nephew and a dedicated journal keeper. He gave them enough supplies for a month and an order to follow the Yass River down until it met the Murrumbidgee.

Still they didn't find it. But they were the first known white men to stumble across the very part of the plains where Canberra's fractured city heart, Civic, stands today.

Throsby Smith's journal entry for 7 December 1820, reads:

> Ascending a Stony Range, Barren and Scrubby; at 11 on the top of the hill; some beautiful clear plain in sight, bearing S. by E.; and extensive chain of mountains running S.S.E. and N.N.W. … we then descended the range into a scrubby country for about ½ a mile, then into a most beautiful forest country, gentle hills and valleys well watered by streams, and a fine rich Black Soil. Came on to

> one of the plains, we saw at 11 o'clock. At ½ past 1, came to a very extensive plain, fine Rich Soil and plenty of grass. Came to a beautiful river that was running thro' the plains in a S.W. direction, by the side of which we slept that night. When we made the Hut this evening, we saw several pieces of stone ... which proved to be limestone.

On 8 December, he wrote:

> At Daylight, ... Myself and Vaughan set out down the river in S.W. direction for the purpose of ascertaining which way the waters went; at 10 o'clock we ascended a very high hill from the top of which we had an extensive view all round; and, finding the waters still continue to run in a S.W. direction, we declined going down the River. We then returned to the hut, and staid for the Night; the Banks of the River on both sides, the whole of the way we went which was a distance of near 10 miles, is a most beautiful forest as far as we could see, thinly wooded by Gums and Bastard Box, the tops of the Hills stony and Stone Sand, but in the valleys a fine Rich Soil.

Writing in 1927, Dr Frederick Watson, a trustee

of the Public Library of New South Wales and the editor of thirty-three volumes of transcribed 'significant' documents on Australia's colonial past, concluded Wild and his companions had stepped on the future site of the Australian capital.

'Wild and his companions crossed the low ridge of hills which separates the watersheds of the Yass and Molonglo Rivers. From one of these hills, they observed the Canberra Plains, and, after crossing these plains, camped somewhere near Duntroon. In the evening, they discovered the deposits of limestone, which gave the first name to the district – Limestone Plains.' The 'very high hill' Throsby Smith and Vaughan ascended was Black Mountain, Watson presumes, and on 'the 9th December, Wild and his companions, the discoverers of Canberra, travelled direct to the southern end of Lake George where they had camped seven days previously and returned thence to the settled districts'.

In late March 1821 Throsby made another journey south from Lake George. Watson says that while he finally found the Murrumbidgee during this trip, he didn't record precisely when in his journal.

Watson concludes: 'It is certain, however, that he travelled over the site of Canberra; that he traced the Molonglo River towards its junction with the Murrumbidgee, and that he discovered the Murrumbidgee.'

Every day after I've walked up the acute saddle of Red Hill, I stop to catch breath at the Davidson Trig that stands precisely in the middle of the range. I never tire of the view as I look out towards the north-eastern reach of the Molonglo, which is about where Throsby had stood. There were a few trees then. But there's millions more across the plains today, planted over a century to fill in the old sheep paddock where the city began.

Throsby retired to his station, Throsby Park, in the Southern Highlands. Most early histories assert that his 'general health' was poor for years – a more genteel way, perhaps, of saying he was psychologically frail. Macquarie had appointed him to the colony's new legislative assembly. But Throsby was under other pressure. In 1811 he had acted as guarantor for the mortgage on a ship purchased by his friend, Garnham Blaxcell. Blaxcell disappeared inexplicably in 1817, saddling Throsby with his debt. The Supreme Court ordered Throsby to pay principal and interest totalling £4000.

Aged fifty-one, on 2 April 1828, Throsby shot himself dead.

In May 1823 Wild led a final expedition south from Lake George, through the cleft of two prominent northern hills and across the Limestone Plains. Accompanied by Captain Mark Currie of the Royal Navy and Captain John Ovens, after crossing the plains he went further south and through a steep valley. The trio emerged at yet another vast expanse of open land. In honour of the daughter of Major General Sir Thomas Brisbane, recently appointed governor, the military men named the wide flat valley that stretched before them 'Isabella's Plain'.

To the Ngambri it had long been Tuggeranong – 'Cold Valley'. It is Tuggeranong today, too – the southernmost town centre of the ACT. Stretching before the majestic blue line of the Brindabella mountain range, it is a place of sprawling suburbs, of big, modern homes with hedges of *Callistemon, Grevillea, Pittosporum* and *Escallonia.* The suburbs are surrounded by greenbelts of sometimes unconnected bush and grasslands that simultaneously attract the birds and confuse the 'roos, who are massacred nightly on the roads that wind through them.

In the end, Brisbane's daughter, Isabella Maria, didn't get the whole plain – just a suburb that stands close to the centre of 'Nappy Valley', as Tuggeranong was somewhat sneeringly dubbed in the 1970s by the Canberra establishment of the old inner south. 'Nappy Valley', because the builders and other tradesmen drawn to Canberra by the public servants who wanted to renovate a bit of Balmain, Fitzroy or West End into their south-facing bungalows and cottages in Forrest, Griffith, Red Hill, Narrabundah, Ainslie, Reid, Braddon and Turner, settled there. They escaped the oppressive expense of the big cities. They came, they built and they raised children in their own little bit of bush bliss. Other, more progressive Canberra professionals, unfazed by pretensions of class or some illusory inner-city lifestyle, easily settled for the valley's bucolic charms too.

In more recent decades the inner-city dwellers – perhaps while driving through the no longer so new southern suburbs for Saturday soccer, or maybe on the way to the skifields – realised something had changed. Out there in Nappy Valley, beneath a wintry blanket of mist and wood smoke from thousands of Coonaras, lived Canberra's new dominant middle class. They drove new SUVs, sent their kids to the grammar schools – and holidayed at Thredbo and Perisher. For some time the Nappy Valley had even been encroaching on the South Coast of New South Wales, its residents snapping up bargain basement holiday shacks with million-dollar views after John Howard sacked thousands of Canberra public servants who had no choice but to liquidate their chattels. So good is life in what was Nappy Valley (the babies have themselves grown into parents) that the senior public servants have now moved in too.

In the past few years, Tuggeranong town centre has claimed elements of what an inner-city Canberra might have been. With its picturesque lake edged by medium-density, energy-efficient apartments, restaurants, cafés, bars and specialty shops, Tuggeranong has developed a coherent centre – a heartbeat and a genuine street life.

But this is a digression by almost two centuries from the discovery by Ovens, Currie and Wild of the Cold Valley.

Currie and Ovens wrote that by the time they reached the Limestone Plains the last white settlement stood about five days behind them. This would make the settled frontier somewhere about Gundaroo.

By some accounts the first settlers and livestock did not arrive until as late as 1826. But it seems likely that the first rudimentary huts were erected in late 1823 on land at Acton, on the banks of the Molonglo where the National Museum of Australia and parts of the Australian National University are situated today.

The huts belonged to Joshua John Moore, a retired lieutenant of the 14th Regiment of Foot.

Today's Ngambri elders say thousands of their people lived on the plains at that time and met at Acton for corroborees.

Moore, who fought at the Battle of Waterloo in 1815, arrived in Australia aboard the *Elizabeth* in October 1816. Having served as registrar of the Governor's Court and on the Supreme Court, he was granted land by Macquarie near Cabramatta (south-western Sydney) and later Goulburn.

About the same time, Campbell set about claiming the land and sheep that he was awarded in compensation for the lost ship.

He sent his 'man', the enigmatic 'Captain' James Ainslie – a fellow Scot who most of the earliest Canberra historians insist was another Waterloo veteran – to collect the sheep and set up a station on the southern frontier.

In a speech to the Royal Australian Historical Society in 1922, historian Henry Selkirk painted a vivid picture of Ainslie as the archetypal tough pioneer.

Ainslie is widely said to have been a trooper in the 2nd Dragoons (Royal Scots Greys), one of the heavy cavalry units that fought at Waterloo. After the victory they were at the vanguard of British cavalry that pursued the fleeing French.

That is where, according to Selkirk, 'Ainslie found himself single-handed in pursuit of a detached party of French cavalry'.

> The latter, recovering from their first panic, and finding that their pursuer was unsupported, suddenly wheeled around and attacking Ainslie left him *hors-de-combat* as the result of a sabre cut across his head. In spite of his damaged skull, Ainslie ultimately recovered, but was ever afterwards subject, under severe excitement, to violent fits of frenzy.

Silkirk said 'soon after' the return of the Currie and Ovens expedition to Sydney in 1823, Ainslie took delivery of Campbell's '6000 ewes' at Bathurst.

Selkirk says Ainslie went on to Yass, where he met a tribe of Aboriginal people 'from whom he ascertained that some thirty miles southerly there was a large extent of good open grazing country. Guided by one of the gins, he ultimately reached the Molonglo River, at a spot known by the natives as "Pialligo," where he established the sheep station in Campbell's name'.

The true story is more nuanced. It was October 1825 when Ainslie collected the sheep in Bathurst and, with his convict labourers, headed to Goulburn. The Goulburn settlers insisted there was no land left and directed him to Boorowa, where there were only blacks and kangaroos. When he arrived in Boorowa, Ainslie and his sheep encountered a tribe of terrified Aboriginal people. They had never seen a Caucasian man or sheep before. Some ran into the scrub. Others ran up trees. To them, the white Ainslie was the spirit of a dead black man, for a black man's spirit was always white. With his other ragged dirty spirits in chains and his white fluffy four-legged creatures, Ainslie was a terrifying sight.

What could they do?

They decided to sacrifice a Ngambri woman who they'd earlier stolen from down on the plains.

They told her they'd kill her unless she led this spirit away.

According to the story as passed down through the descendants of the original inhabitants, she led him south-east to the only other place she knew – Ngambri country. As they rounded the base of the great mountain they stopped at a lone, very old and flourishing yellow box redgum – one of the Ngambri's corroboree trees – that was fed by a spring. (The tree is still there today in Corroboree Park, Ainslie.) It offered the last shade on the north of the plains. They camped there. Later they followed the river east.

Ainslie gesticulated – 'Where are we?'

'Bialgi,' (*Be seated*) she said. Phonetically, it sounded like 'pialligo'. And that's what it became.

Pialligo would become one of Canberra's accidental unpolished gems. It began as the food basket, the location of the settlement's earliest market gardens and orchards.

Today, it is where the city's gardeners (to live in Canberra is to garden) buy their shrubs, trees and vegetable seedlings, their trellis, pots and composting lime. It has a pottery, a few horse agistments, several fine restaurants, cafés, the obligatory gift shops and a winery. But nestled on the river flat between the airport, a bend in the turbid Molonglo and the back of semi-industrial Fyshwick, Pialligo looks more like a workaday town in the British Midlands or Wales than it does the faux and chintzy craft villages that have sprung up elsewhere around the capital region.

Pialligo's casual sprawl is almost anathema to the rest of Canberra, with its defined order. That, along with its colours and its fragrances – the soft golden and red hues of the European trees and cherry blossoms contrasted with the verdant natives; apples and coffee, sizzling bacon, fertilised earth, horse manure and piss – account for Pialligo's untidy charm and beauty.

After the Molonglo flooded in 2010, the city's authorities began removing the dense copses of ancient willows whose cephalopod roots had burrowed deep into the banks. For generations, their branches had formed a dark canopy along the waterway's shores. I watched as the contractors in their luminous safety vests started their saws. The pitch of the machines changed from a whine to a throaty growl as the blades ripped through the willows' grey crocodile-skin bark and easily into the moist white flesh of the trunks. The weeping willow is a noxious weed around here. They had to go. But I wondered as I watched from the highway across the river, if the contractors – or anyone – knew anything about the trees' ancestral line.

I wondered, because earlier that day in the National Library of Australia I'd stumbled across a reference to the provenance of the trees. In 1823 a ship en route to Australia stopped at the island of St Helena, a British protectorate in the South Atlantic Ocean that is best known as the home in exile for Napoleon Bonaparte, who spent his final years there after defeat at Waterloo. After Napoleon died in 1821 he was buried for the best part of twenty years in St Helena's Valley of the Willows (his body was eventually moved to Paris and entombed at Les Invalides).

One of the ship's passengers cut slips from a willow overshadowing Napoleon's grave and kept them alive for the rest of the voyage by sticking the ends into potatoes. Napoleon's willows are said to have flourished in the colony – especially along the Molonglo at Pialligo and at Acton, where Elijah Bainbridge planted offshoots of the original Napoleonic slips in 1854. So the story goes, according to the tabloid pen of old John Gale, who seems to be its secondary source. It may well be true; Gale would have known Bainbridge. For beyond the embellishments, and notwithstanding his great storyteller's embrace of yowies, the supernatural and the inexplicable, there is a kernel of truth in most of Gale's best yarns.

The Molonglo's shores are now sunlit and clear. The willows now fuel Canberra's fireplaces and pizza ovens. Pialligo has lost most of that which had been its signature tree for the best part of two centuries.

But the determinedly idiosyncratic Pialligo has always, quite appropriately, been of ambiguous identity.

According to Frederick Slater, an early expert on the origins of Canberra names, the response of Ainslie's Ngambri guide to his question about their whereabouts might have simply meant 'I'll tell you by and by'.

'But there is no record that she ever returned with the desired information, and Pialligo it has remained until this day.' Slater was close to the true story: be seated, and wait a while, mean much the same thing. Regardless, it is close to where Ainslie built a small hut of stone and wood, Limestone

Cottage, said to be for a time the southernmost house in the world with glazed windows.

Selkirk said,

> Here Ainslie erected his huts and ruled his little settlement in true military fashion, mustering his hands day by day and giving his orders as though dealing with a company of soldiers. While maintaining strict discipline he had the happy faculty of securing the confidence of those under him, and consequently had little trouble in dealing with his staff of assigned servants.

Ainslie seemed the near-perfect frontiersman. He could masterfully handle gun, axe and horse, was resourceful, unafraid of the bush and formed very close relationships with the local tribes. He was respected as a fair convict overseer and good boss of free men in his employ. But Ainslie drank. And when drunk he became wildly unpredictable and frightening.

Selkirk continued,

> Like other mortals, Ainslie had his failings, and at times was wont to indulge not wisely but too well in the real Jamaica rum of the period. On these

> occasions ... the old soldier would seize his gun, and with the light of battle in his eyes, commence a furious fusillade directed at the trunks of the adjacent gum trees, in which he seemed to recognise his ancient enemies at Waterloo. It is not difficult to believe that at such moments his employees voted Ainslie in his cups as one whose room was better than his company.

Canberra's early histories, most of which were published about the time that the capital was named in 1913 or when federal Parliament moved to the fledgling city in 1927, overlooked Aboriginal dispossession and the complex, fraught relationships between blacks and the pioneers.

Watson made a curious mention in his *Brief History* of the early bushrangers Dublin Jack and William Tenant robbing Limestone Cottage. It seems odd that he should write that the bushrangers 'called at and robbed a hut occupied by James Ainslie, R. Campbell's overseer, and an aboriginal'. Here Watson alludes to Ainslie's personal circumstance but wilfully evades any meaningful detail.

For Ainslie lived with the young Aboriginal woman, Ija Ngambri, who had led him to Pialligo.

They even had a child together, Ju.nin.mingo – or Nanny – in 1827. Ainslie's partner was mentioned little at the time or by the first historians to tell his story. To them she was 'Ainslie's lubra'. It was not a situation Ainslie's contemporaries or those who came soon after cared to highlight; white women were scarce, some settlers took black women as unofficial partners out of physical and domestic need.

Ija Ngambri's descendant, Shane Mortimer, confirms she lived with Ainslie and Nanny in Limestone Cottage until Ainslie vanished.

Ainslie ran the sheep station Duntroon for the Campbells until the mid-1830s, turning a modest flock of 710 sheep into more than 20,000 (after sales). It was long enough for the steep mountain at Duntroon's north to take his name. Then he disappeared. None of the white histories have adequately explained what happened to Ainslie or his descendants after he went.

Did he, I wonder, take Ija Ngambri and Nanny? The answer is no.

Gale, in his *Canberra History and Legends,* recounted one story of Ainslie's death and burial on his own mountain.

> Ainslie, a good fellow in all other respects, was a hard drinker. Probably this besetment led to him leaving the army. Be that as it may, he and his men were on the top of this particular eminence [Mount Ainslie] one day, and, fuddled by drink, Ainslie accepted a bet of a bottle of rum that he would ride his horse full gallop down its most precipitous slope ... Poor Ainslie essayed his self-imposed task, but never accomplished it. His horse fell with its rider, whose neck was broken. Seeing he was dead, his body was buried where he fell – but regrettably 'no man knoweth' the locality of his burial to this day.

That Ainslie died on his own mountain was but one of the apocryphal stories that grew around him. For Ainslie was apparently less than he – and the early Canberra historians – made out. According to Rowan Henderson, the curator of social history at the Canberra Museum and Gallery, Ainslie was not among the 37,000 British servicemen of all ranks who received the Waterloo Medal – awarded to all soldiers who fought at the Battle of Ligny (16 June 1815), the Battle of Quatre Bras (16 June 1815) or at Waterloo (18 June 1815). This casts serious doubt on whether he actually fought – and received the notorious head wound that, mixed with drink, rendered him so erratic – at Waterloo.

Henderson's research established that Ainslie and Campbell fell out after Ainslie set up an illegal liquor store on the Limestone Plains. Ainslie fled to Liverpool on the *Edinburgh* in March 1835, and then to Kelso in Scotland, where he reunited with the son, James, who he'd left behind as an infant when he sailed to New South Wales. In Kelso he told stories of his frequent clashes with bush-rangers and natives in Australia that, he claimed, had resulted in cuts and gunshot wounds to his head and body. Court records indicate Ainslie was violent, unpredictable and possibly insane – and often a drunken public nuisance. Henderson's research disclosed that after being apprehended for one of many alleged assaults, Ainslie hanged him-self in prison on 11 April 1844.

Campbell increasingly spent his time at Dun-troon after the death in 1833 of his wife Agnes. By this time he had significantly increased, through purchase and further government grant, his share-holding on the plains to the maximum allowable of some 2500 acres. In the 1830s he was permitted to buy another 8000 acres, making him the biggest owner of the best land on the Limestone Plains. Campbell named the property Duntroon in deference to his ancestral home, Duntroon Castle, which stands on the shores of Loch Crinan in Argyll.

The heart of Robert Campbell's home still beats as the Officers' Mess of the Royal Military College. My guide, an affable lieutenant colonel, leads me through the gardens and into the old house. Robert Campbell and his sons Charles and George had aimed to fill the gardens with as many exotic trees and plants as possible.

A rose garden flourished from early on. So, too, did the English-style lawn, top-dressed and hand-clipped so that it rolled down from the veranda, like a soft green carpet, to the untamed bush beyond. Today, the lawn hints at croquet, tippety run, shuttlecock and garden parties amid the azaleas, roses, pepper tree and the Canary Island date palm, a late addition. On the walls of the house, photographs of the homestead's gentlemen and ladies portray an oasis of charmed, gentrified existence remote from the general hardships of the plains.

We pass, appropriately, a painting of the Battle

of Waterloo, all rearing horses and sabres drawn.

A washed-out sepia image shows a croquet party, circa 1872, posing on the grass. There is George Campbell and his wife Marianne, and their daughter Sophia. My officer-guide leads me into the main bedroom, and opens the shutters onto a small balcony, below which is the scene of the photograph. Sophia is said to have fallen or to have been pushed from this balcony. She died of serious head injuries. It's rumoured she was either in love with a gardener, forbidden by her father George to marry him, spurned by him or pregnant to him (or a combination of all four). Each proposition can be disproved.

But Sophia's ghost, my lieutenant colonel tells me, is said to haunt the homestead. Not that he believes in ghosts. But some officers refuse to stay in the old place – and strange things (unexplained chills; someone inexplicably pinned to the bed; night-time bumps; unexplained movement of objects – the usual paranormal stuff) have happened there.

We go back downstairs and inspect the paintings on the walls of the dining room. In 1870 Duntroon and its gardens were painted from up on Mount Pleasant, showing the plains bare of trees but for a few willows on the brown, barely flowing river. Later paintings depict Duntroon's flourishing gardens and the homestead as the nucleus of a bustling village. There's stock on fields around the river. In 1914 – four years after the Commonwealth had established the college, having already compulsorily acquired the Campbell land – there's cattle all over the plains, and fences too. That is what Canberra looked like when the politicians finally settled upon it for a capital.

Now it is very much a military village. The service chiefs live in the immaculately restored old homesteads that surround Duntroon House. Children play on the lawn outside the childcare centre. In the conservatory, the officers gather for morning tea. Some know a little about the old place. They all know that Duntroon is probably more notorious these days for the wrong reasons – scandals involving officer cadets and bastardisation. It's unfair, really, because the Duntroon military establishment has its own rich history of culture, academia and, of course, sacrifice, in every foreign conflict involving Australia. Duntroon's first commander, Major General Sir William Bridges, fatally wounded at Gallipoli, is buried high on the rise behind his college. His grave became critical to

Canberra's evolution and layout. But that is a story for later.

Ainslie's earliest immediate neighbour was Joshua John – J.J. – Moore. Yet Moore's shepherds arrived up to two years before Ainslie.

On 16 December 1826, Moore wrote to the authorities saying he wanted to buy the land on which he was already running stock, 'my having had possession of that land for upwards of three years'.

Moore wrote that his huts and stockyards were already on the land.

'The land which I wish to purchase is situate at Canberray. On the E. Bank of the River which waters Limestone Plains, above its junction with the Murrumbeeja, adjoining the grant of Mr Robert Campbell, Senr.'

The letter attaches Moore's name to the choicest part of the plains from at least late 1823. It also appears to be one of the first recorded official mentions of the name 'Canberray', which would become Canberra. By 1833, Campbell was undoubtedly the biggest residential landholder. But he was neither the first to run stock nor the first to use the names from which 'Canberra' derived in relation to his holdings.

In 1831, after the colony's surveyor general had noted that the land Moore wanted was south of an arbitrary line beyond which settlers were not allowed to select, Moore wrote: 'I am desirous of retaining the Thousand Acres of Land already in my possession, situate in the County of Murray, on the Molonglo River, it is called and known by the name of Canburry, and is bounded on the South by the Molonglo River, and on the West by Canburry Creek.'

Selkirk pointed out that 'in his correspondence Moore is scrupulously precise in his expressions, as a result, no doubt, of his military and legal training'.

> In using the words 'called and known as Canburry,' he evidently desires to make it quite clear that this is not a name given by himself, no new name, but one that had been and was generally recognised. Now Moore is referring to land first occupied by him as a stock station in the year 1823, the same year in which Captain Curry made his exploration southerly; moreover, he refers to it as bearing the local name of 'Canberry', afterwards corrected to

> 'Canburry.' If, then, in the very earliest pioneering days this name existed, how is its origins to be accounted for unless from an aboriginal source? Indeed, this would appear to be the only reasonable explanation, and the fact of Mr Moore's correction of his original spelling would seem to be an attempt on his part to convey more precisely the intonation of the word as he had received it phonetically.

Vigorous pedantic debate about the genesis of 'Canberra' would preoccupy columnists, historians and obsessive letter-writers for decades.

'Canberra is, without any doubt, a native name,' wrote Frederick Robinson in *Canberra's First Hundred Years,* in 1924.

> Nor is there any doubt that in pronunciation it should be accented on the first syllable, and almost omit the 'e' in the second. A happily illiterate witness to a marriage in 1840 wrote the name phonetically as he knew it and spelt it 'Canbrey'. This is good evidence! The uncertain quality of the middle and final vowels of the name, as evidenced by the varied spellings – Canberry, Canburry, Canbury, Canberra, is also easily explained from its aboriginal origin. The

> Australian native, according to one graphical description, 'spat out his words like tobacco chews'; in addition he also burred his Rs more fiercely than a Scotchman. Under these circumstances the exact nature of a vowel before or after an R is a fighting problem for trained phoneticians.

Leading the argument for the negative in the 1930s, Frederick Slater wrote: 'No amount of juggling with the spelling of Canberra can give it an aboriginal origin.'

I want to get closer to the truth, so I meet Shane Mortimer at the National Museum at Acton – appropriately, he says, because long before and after the pioneer J.J. Moore started grazing there, the site of the musem was a sacred corroboree ground.

He explains that since the High Court's 1992 Mabo decision, the Ngambri have had Common Law Native Title for the whole ACT. That strikes me as delightfully allegoric given his heritage; Mortimer is a direct descendant of Ija Ngambri, the Aboriginal woman who led Ainslie from Boorowa down on to the river at Pialligo.

James Ainslie is his great, great, great, great grandfather.

The museum is the repository of national treasures and the custodian of great responsibility. Curator and anthropologist Mike Pickering has shown me pieces of the museum's vast collection that includes indigenous skeletons originally collected by Professor Colin MacKenzie at the Institute of Anatomy. The museum is charged with repatriating the bodies, many of which were collected from rural properties on MacKenzie's behalf by George Murray Black. I see something of the responsibility. And Pickering also shows me many treasures: convict love pennies; a vast collection of Aboriginal weapons; breast plates given to Aboriginal 'kings'; children's drawings; medical equipment from Kenmore Mental Hospital; animal embryos; human organs in jars; leg irons; a piece of lens from the Mount Stromlo telescope destroyed in the bushfires; the *Play School* flower clock; Ned Kelly's Jerilderie Letter; Joseph Banks prints; Billy Hughes' office furniture, and so on.

Before the museum was built, it was the original site, from 1914, of Canberra Hospital, a curiously revered place that in 1997 was going to be destroyed at a public 'implosion'. But the event became symbolic of government incompetence and the shortcomings of economic rationalism; the company hired to destroy the hospital cut costs, creating an explosion that rained shrapnel down upon thousands of spectators. Metal struck a little girl in the head. She died horribly.

I ask Mortimer: 'Canberra comes from Ngambri, right?'

'Correct.'

'So, what does Ngambri actually mean?'

'Cleavage.'

'You sure?'

Mortimer smiles.

'No doubt whatsoever. Her womb is where Capital Hill is today.'

In the 1830s the main settlements comprised a few huts and stockyards (the days of the grand homesteads were still some way off). There were no fences, so the stock roamed under the charge of the shepherds, who lived in rudimentary humpies. Most labourers were ticket-of-leave men or convicts.

By 1833, eight stations operated between Ginninderra in the north and the Molonglo. There were about seven more at Lake George and Bungendore and Gundaroo.

In the same year, the white population of the County of Murray – stretching from Yass to Micalago and from the Upper Murrumbidgee to the Shoalhaven – was 510. There were 475 men (315 of them bonded and 160 free) and 35 women, of whom 33 were free. There were 327 Protestants and 183 Roman Catholics.

A young Anglican priest, the Reverend Edward Smith, became the first holy man of the plains. From 1838, the landowners paid him to minister to the homesteads. In 1839 Smith complained that while he had found a jail, there was no school or church.

> I am anxious to add word respecting the moral state of the District, so far as it has come under my own observation. There being no Schools the children are growing up in ignorance, and the men are for the most part hardened in iniquity. But what can be expected when they have been so long without the means of Grace?

The squires were sympathetic. In 1841 Reverend Smith laid the foundation stone for St John's Anglican Church, on a small piece of land on the edge of Duntroon. Campbell donated the land and paid for the church, built of sandstone taken from Black Mountain and Quarry Hill in Yarralumla.

Campbell also donated one hundred acres for use as a 'glebe' (a farm to support the vicarage and church community), while two acres were allocated for the church grounds and cemetery.

St John's was consecrated in 1845, the church register locating it at 'Canbury'. From 1852, the church regarded itself 'of Canberra'. It may not have been the Limestone Plains' first institution (the prison at Acton probably has that privilege), but St John's was the first institution to claim the name 'Canberra'.

If a single place represents this city's pioneering history, it must be St John's. I've found one or two buildings in the territory that may have been built earlier, but they were purely utilitarian – barns and stables. St John's was constructed with prescience to become the nucleus of a community.

A giant tree tells its story from both inside and out. The trunk's tawny concentric rings record droughts, floods and fires, its bark, the human interference and the lives of the insects and animals to which it's been home. St John's offers up its narrative in a similar fashion. Campbell's sandstone building gives way to bluestone where his son, George, extended the nave. The walls are punctuated with plaques in bronze and stone marking the names of worshipping pioneers. Outside, under gnarly oaks and conifers, lie the people who built the church, cleared the plains and dreamt of a 'continuing city'.

Australians are familiar with St John's Anglican Church.

But most wouldn't realise it.

During Kevin Rudd's two-and-a-half-year prime ministership, he regularly chose St John's as the backdrop – a political stage – for his weekend pronouncements on everything from the vacuousness of the Liberal Party leadership to the great moral challenge of climate change mitigation.

The cameras framed Rudd through the rustic portico gate as he strode with his wife towards them along the path. Then the cameras would pan wider and deeper to incorporate the elegant blonde Gothic Revival spire with its hilltop-shaped stained-glass windows and its deep entrance arch of entrance – added to the church in 1878. In the cutaways, you might glimpse, off to the left, the whitewash of the city's first schoolhouse or a tombstone the hue of weathered ivory.

The voice-over on these stories would inevitably describe Rudd as having been 'outside church in Canberra today'.

In 1851, when lightning struck the little church, it stood alone on the tree-less plains. It now stands in the middle of Reid, one of Canberra's original suburbs whose gentrified bungalows sit on big, proudly lawned allotments. Reid's publicly planted streets and neat houses were an early showcase for the new capital.

On 20 August 1851 the first full-time vicar, Reverend George Gregory, twenty-five, drowned in the Molonglo after visiting the plains' southern homesteads.

The Sydney Morning Herald of 28 August 1851 reported 'an unusual gloom has been cast over our little community by the untimely death of Rev. George Gregory, Minister of St John's, Canbury, who was drowned last Wednesday ... while attempting to swim across the Queanbeyan or Molonglo River.' The report continued:

> During his absence from home the rivers in this quarter had risen considerably above their

> usual height, but Mr Gregory, who was a very good swimmer, after calling at the residence of Mr Mowle, JP, where he dined, expressed his determination to cross to the Parsonage, which is on the opposite bank. The current was so strong that Mr Mowle and another gentleman urged him strongly not to make the attempt. Mr Gregory, however, persisted … and he, after taking off his coat and boots, sprang into the river with a smile. The force of the current hurried him down the stream, but at first he did not seem alarmed, and called out to Mr Mowle: 'All's right.' Almost immediately after he suddenly sank.

They buried Gregory in his own churchyard in a vault belonging to the Campbells. Curiously, Robert Campbell, who died in 1846 while sitting in his European garden at Duntroon, was buried at Parramatta. But most of his children and many grandchildren, including Sophia, are in St John's yard.

Gregory's successor, Pierce Galliard-Smith, served the parish for fifty years. He planted thousands of trees in the grounds and about the glebe. There is a plaque inside St John's commemorating Galliard-Smith, who died in 1908, and to the son he raised in the parish, William Bradshaw Galliard-Smith. William joined the 2nd Scottish Horse and died in the Battle of Bakenlaagte in the Boer War.

The St John's cemetery grew with Galliard-Smith's trees as the next generation of pioneering families consolidated their landholdings and inter-married. Meanwhile, more new free men, some already with wives and children, kept arriving to work on the original settlers' land.

A rusted wrought-iron fence surrounds the Campbell plot – the largest but not the most elaborate in the churchyard. It denotes Scottish pragmatism and functionality more than sentiment.

It's a steamy mid-summer afternoon when I visit for the fifth time. There's not a breath of wind and the sky is pregnant with gunmetal clouds, groaning and cracking under weight. Thunder comes from the south-west, reverberating first off the Brindabellas, Mugga Mugga and Red Hill before rolling north across the plains and mountains and echoing in waves about the gravestones. The lightning forks horizontally just beneath the cloudy blanket, momentarily illuminating the dim corners of the cemetery, like a flash gun in a cellar. A dozen crows, their feathery overcoats oily in the moist air, bounce frenetically about and then stop suddenly to voice their harrowing cries, as if electrified by so much atmospheric static.

A misty patina of rain comes as I stand before the Campbell plot. Someone has left a small bunch of blue and turquoise hydrangeas. The jagged stems vary dramatically in length as if snapped from one of those glorious Reid gardens either by a child or someone ancient. The flowers rest on the pine needles and moss, unadorned beyond a small piece of mauve ribbon tied into a rudimentary single-looped bow. Whoever left the flowers has also left open the gate in the heavy iron fence. I don't know why, but I close it and then shelter under a towering nearby conifer.

The rain sets in. The water adds definition to the work of the stonemasons whose words have eroded under decades of baking sun, blasting wind, sleet, rain and snow. And so the rain teases out the names of the dead: among them Palmer, Crace, Gibbes, Schumack, Webb, Guise, Ginn and Blundell.

A simple headstone records the death of Joe Blundell on 13 February 1874. But there's no hint at all as to his life, which began in 1798 in Thurnham, England. In 1825 a gamekeeper caught Joe and his mate Samuel Knight poaching. Blundell nearly beat the gamekeeper to death with the butt of his gun. A constable arrested him outside the Rose and Crown pub in nearby Maidstone as Blundell carried a sack holding three pheasants. He escaped through the roof of the jail. But Joe left a trail that led directly to the bed of a young woman. The constables saw his boots protruding from the bedcovers. It was a ruse; Joe was caught, hiding in the chimney. He was found guilty. The judge ordered him to hang. But the sentence was commuted to life in the colony. He arrived in Port Jackson in 1826.

Blundell won his ticket of leave in 1834 despite having absconded from his master in 1831 with a married free woman, Mercy Blanch, and her baby John. The cuckolded husband had a warrant issued against Blundell for robbery and offered a £5 reward. But the couple went to ground for a decade then turned up on the Limestone Plains in 1843. Joe began work for the Campbells as a bullock-driver. His elder sons, including George, also worked with the Campbells' bullock teams. Joe and his wife 'Susan Osborne' (Blanch) built a hut on a small mound on Duntroon overlooking the Molonglo known as Blundell's Hill. There they raised their eleven children.

Joe's cottage is long gone; a 39-metre-tall

Canadian flagpole on the edge of the lake marks the spot where it once stood. From there, though, signs still point to 'Blundell's Cottage', which today stands further around on the northern shore of the lake between the Commonwealth and Kings Avenue bridges. But Joe and Susan never lived in the five-room stone cottage. The Campbells built it for their ploughman, William Ginn, in 1858. Joe's son George moved in with his wife Flora in 1874. They stayed for almost fifty years.

Joe seemed to seize the backhanded opportunity that transportation offered him. With the exception of 'stealing' another man's wife, Joe – who died with ninety-three grandchildren – was largely law abiding.

Other transportees who lived on the Limestone Plains found abiding by colonial laws more challenging.

Isaac Beaumont of Yorkshire was originally sentenced to hang for highway robbery in 1837. Beaumont, though not yet twenty and already a father, had his sentence commuted to transportation for life, arriving in Australia in 1838. He was freed in 1845 and worked for a wealthy landholder, Henry Antill, on a property near the Molonglo. In 1844, while employed on another Antill property at Picton in the Southern Highlands, he married Mary Ann Whitelaw, a free immigrant and house servant.

In 1856 Mary Ann died while delivering the couple's seventh child. Something in Beaumont snapped. He fell in with the 'Jingera Mob'. Named with reference to the Jingera Ranges that run between Queanbeyan and Braidwood, the gang was a loose alignment of cattle thieves, escaped convicts, hardened bushrangers and other assorted misfits and drunks.

In 1862 the police charged Beaumont with pig stealing. Two years later, by then a hardened bushranger, he was charged with Highway Robbery and sentenced to ten years' hard labour. Presiding magistrate Thomas Ruttledge wrote that Beaumont was among the worst characters in the district. Somehow the children survived without either Isaac or their mother.

Beaumont returned, broken, to the district after serving his sentence. He died in 1896.

With eighteen children between them, it was almost inevitable that the Blundells and the Beaumonts would be linked by marriage.

Today, their descendants are scattered well beyond the Limestone Plains.

One who stayed is Allan Hawke, a former Commonwealth department head, prime ministerial chief of staff and senior diplomat.

'I'm five generations down from them now – all in this area. They were both convicts, so my heritage – and I suppose arguably the country too – has benefited from that English practice of exporting some of its very best talent to the colony,' Hawke says.

'I often wonder how they ended up so differently: Blundell came here and went straight and Beaumont went bushranging.'

Just over to the right, under another gnarly old pine tree, stands the oldest stone in the cemetery. It names six members of the Guise family from three generations. Yet in all likelihood seven Guises are buried here.

Patriarch Richard Guise was born in Lorraine, France, in 1757. Supposedly of royal blood, he fled to England just before the revolutionaries stormed the Bastille in 1789, and joined the Royal Grenadier Horse Guards. He married a young Englishwoman, Elizabeth, and joined the New South

Wales Corps, and the pair arrived in Australia a few years after the First Fleet. Guise was in the Corps during the Rum Rebellion and the governorships of Hunter, King and Bligh. By 1809, he was running the Jolly Sailor, a squalid Sydney pub.

Richard Guise died in 1821. His adult sons were granted land at Gundaroo and Bywong west of Lake George – apparently for helping Throsby to push his roads into the interior from the Southern Highlands and Bathurst. By 1845 the family owned 280 000 acres around Gundaroo.

Richard's elderly widow Elizabeth lived on one family property there. So, too, did her granddaughter, Mary Ann, who had married George Brownlow, a man the Guise family considered an outsider of low moral standing, a womaniser and a fortune hunter who was eager to sell his wife's share of the Guise estate.

Brownlow was a nasty drunk and an abusive husband.

One night in April 1855, Mary Ann stabbed him with a carving knife during a drunken argument. He died three days later. Mary Ann, pregnant with her third child, was convicted of murder and sentenced to hang. The colony divided over the case as Guise waited on death row at Goulburn

Gaol to give birth before the execution. One of the last things she apparently did before walking to the gallows was breastfeed the infant, George – named after his father.

The correspondent for *Empire* reported:

> She had fallen away considerably during her incarceration … and when brought on to the fatal drop her extremely delicate appearance deeply affected every one present, and caused the tears to start irresistibly from the eyes of the hardiest. Her execution had been fixed to take place at 9 am, but on the previous evening, after the arrival of the mail, and the disappointment of the inhabitants as to its bringing a reprieve, a deputation of the townspeople waited upon the Deputy Sheriff, captain Fitzgerald, and at their earnest solicitation he deferred the fatal hour until 4 o'clock, at the time frankly expressing his opinion that his doing so would be of little service.

But no reprieve came. Mary Ann was taken from her cell and escorted to the foot of the gallows.

> Her interesting countenance, and her severe disability, struck all the beholders with deep

> emotions of pity. Her once fine frame was greatly attenuated, she had to be assisted up the ladder, not from any want of fortitude or resignation, but from sheer enfeeblement of body.

She uttered a final prayer, said 'good bye' and 'patiently surrendered herself to the executioner'.

> The rope was adjusted, the cap drawn over her face, the executioner withdrew the bolt, and falling through the trap door, she was immediately dead without a single struggle or convulsive movement. Every spectator was deeply affected, and stout brave men who would laugh at cannonade, could not with all their efforts control their emotions at the sad, sad sight. After the body had hung a sufficient time it was removed to the cemetery of the Church of England and there interred.

Because she had been executed, the church was not permitted to bury Brownlow in consecrated earth; her remains were interred outside the cemetery proper.

I came across Arnold Thomas, a noted historian of Australian boxing, a few years ago when I was researching a long-dead amateur fighter who had also played football for Collingwood. He told me in passing about the story of Mary Ann Brownlow – his great aunt.

> Her family was deeply distressed that she was buried in Goulburn in unconsecrated ground. It was commonly known around Goulburn at the time – and it still is today – that she was exhumed from the edge of the Church of England cemetery there and taken to St John's in Canberra and entombed in the Guise vault with the rest of her family.

Thomas says that her victim, George Brownlow, is buried in another unmarked grave at St John's.

George, the child Brownlow bore in prison, is said to have died only months after his mother. But descendants are still unsure if that is true.

Mary Ann's brother, Richard Guise, who died on 11 November 1855, was the first person to be buried at St John's.

The second was Sarah Webb, who was buried in what became the Webb family plot, just a few metres away from Richard.

To The Memory of Mrs Sarah Webb who
Giving Birth To Her 10th Child
Departed this Life in 8th November 1845
Leaving a Husband And 6 Children
To lament Her Loss

When their daughter Betsy Celia died at eleven in 1848, Sarah's husband George, a farmer at Uriarra near the Murrumbidgee, had a new stone erected. His name, too, would be added in 1866. In 1848 George had the mason inscribe the stone with the words from St Paul's letter to the Hebrews.

For here have we no continuing city
but seek one to come

Despite losing his wife and at least five children during his lifetime, and despite the daily struggle of life across the Limestone Plains, George Webb chose an epitaph that echoes St Paul's confidence in the capacity of faith to secure the future. Considering Webb's circumstance, I find it a deeply admirable sentiment.

The settlers who followed the Webbs, many churchgoers among them, believed that the words on the stone might be prophetic – even if it would be their children who stood to inherit the prophecy.

Today, they could be rightly impressed by its prescience. The faithful of Canberra still cling to it.

Already an established writer and journalist, it was as a Wesleyan Methodist minister that John Gale arrived in Australia in May 1854. His duties led him to travel widely around Goulburn, Yass and further south on the plains. He quit the ministry in 1857 and in 1860 published the first edition of *The Queanbeyan Age and General Advertiser* – later to become *The Queanbeyan Age*. Besides being an activist proprietor, a great promoter of his home-town, Queanbeyan, and ultimately the most influential proponent of Canberra, Gale was a first-rate yarn spinner and raconteur.

For almost seventy years, Gale documented settlement, basing stories on his own observations and those of other settlers.

Towards the end of Gale's life, in 1929, the owner–proprietor of the *Federal Capital Pioneer*, A.K. Murray, wrote:

> At the ripe age of 97 years, Mr Gale's wonderfully retentive memory surprises all who have had the opportunity to visit him and lead the conversation on events of the past; and when with animated fervour he strikes reminiscent notes, it is surprising to listen to him accurately describing events of fifty, sixty or seventy years ago as though it were but yesterday …

In a preface to Gale's history of the district, published in 1927 to coincide with the opening of Parliament House, Murray wrote: 'Reader you are about to read a work from the pen of the oldest living journalist in the English-speaking world – not forgetting Britain's grand old journalist Thomas Hardy.'

He may have written earlier and for longer – and even outlived – Hardy. But Gale was hardly a comparable stylist.

What he had, however, was an acute eye for the quirky, the bizarre, the spooky – and the compelling. He applied a tabloid sensibility to history and contemporary happenings on the Limestone Plains through his thousands of newspaper columns and his book. His love of the place is evident through his description of his first sight of the plains from Kurrajong Hill, the rise that would in 1988 become the site of the present Parliament House.

> I ascended the stony hill at the foot of which I had landed. Climbing its precipitous slope, I reined in my nag for a twofold reason – that he needed to get his wind, and I, enamoured with the landscape outstretching east and west and south before me, hungrily to feast my eyes upon its varying charms. And where was I standing or rather sitting astride my horse? Close alongside the old kurrajong tree beneath which the Prince of Wales recently laid the foundation-stone of the Federal City's Capitol; lower down its southern slope now stands the Commencement Column, laid with magnificent pomp and ceremony some time before; the lower still, on its eastern foothills, not so long ago, the first sod of Parliament House was turned.

On one of his first visits to Canberra, Gale stayed briefly at Palmerville, which had by then been taken over by William Davis. Davis came to the plains as an overseer for Robert Campbell before working for the Palmers. It is said he transformed the Palmer property into the showcase of the region. Meanwhile, he married one of George T. Palmer's daughters, Suzannah Adriana, and before long bought out her brothers to become squire of Palmerville. Members of the extended Palmer family continued to farm around Gungahlin and Ginninderra.

One hot summer morning I go in search of the village that grew from the Davis property, Ginninderra. I've been told I'll find the heart of old Ginninderra – the homestead, school and store – if I wander around the Gold Creek Village in the suburb of Nicholls. After the Nav Man has steered me through the city and on to the start of the highway to Yass, it guides me finally towards Nicholls. I realise I've been here before – too many times, in fact. For Nicholls is also home to the National Dinosaur Museum (every nation deserves one) and Reptile Park which I visited regularly in the 90s with my eldest daughter.

There's also a faux English pub. Its name – Cockington Green – evokes memories of my father. In his latter years he favoured the counter lunches at Cockington Green; he usually made a point of patronising the pub when he visited us in Canberra.

When I lived in England, I took him for a pint to a 600-year-old pub in a Cornish fishing village. He declared it to be 'just like Cockington Green'.

The old school house is still there all right – converted, these days, into a café. Other original or semi-original buildings of corrugated iron, shingle and stone stand around a dusty courtyard featuring a well and what must be some of the region's oldest gum trees. There's a shop that seemingly sells only crystals.

The school/café is closed. But the door is unlocked so I open it, knock and say 'Hello'. I can hear the hiss and spit of an espresso machine somewhere inside, so I say it again, louder. A man walks towards me. He almost ignores me as I open the door so that he can go past with a coffee for another shopkeeper.

'Hi,' I say. 'I was wondering if I could look inside the school.'

'I'm sorry,' he replies. 'It's a café. It's closed this morning.' So I go into the bookshop. It is stocked with many cardboard boxes of sci-fi and fantasy novels. A woman who is reading one such title studiously ignores me. I poke around the shop, picking up books featuring panel van montages of swords and dragons and Xena Warrior Princess lookalikes with long wispy hair emerging from lakes. More crystals. There's nobody else in the village when I go outside and wander. There's a decrepit old horse-drawn buggy standing under a tree. Maybe it had something to do with the original village, said to have been perhaps the oldest in the Canberra region (Queanbeyan would, I suspect, challenge that). A creaky old cattle dog, its bluey-grey coat mottled and patchy, limps over, cops a whiff, cocks its leg and pisses on the wheel.

Business is booming at the modern stores that orbit and dwarf what remains of old Ginninderra. Tradesmen's utes and family sedans fill the car-park of McDonald's and tourist buses park outside the dinosaur museum, while just beyond the perimeters of Cockington Green a blanket of brown dust, raised by dozens of bulldozers, hangs over the developing suburb of Crace – after Edward Crace, who bought both Gungahlin and Ginninderra from Davis in 1877. Davis and Suzannah – or 'Addie' – had no children. But they concentrated their affections on their nieces and nephews, including Henry Palmer. Henry died while riding Davis's showjumper, Gungarline, at Queanbeyan.

So distraught were they at the loss of their nephew that the couple left the district permanently.

After Davis, respected among free settlers as an employer and an amenable neighbour, Crace was idiosyncratic, litigious and obstinate. He refused to let the residents of nearby properties use 'public' roads through his land. In 1892 he ignored a warning not to cross the flooded Ginninderra Creek, and his horse-drawn carriage became bogged before capsizing in the racing current. Crace and his driver, George Kemp, drowned. Crace's widow Kate stayed in the grand English manor-style Gungahlin homestead until 1915 when the Commonwealth compulsorily acquired it – along with others nearby – for the national capital. Since 1953 the homestead has housed operations of the CSIRO; today the organisation's ecosystem sciences department – including its entomology research – is based there.

From the old Gungahlin homestead you can sense something of what the former squires might have seen. The pastoral plains were uninterrupted but for natural rises and drops: Black Mountain and Mount Ainslie, Mount Majura, Red Hill, Mount Mugga Mugga and the blue Brindabellas as far as the eye could see to the south.

The old Palmer–Davis–Crace property is now sandwiched between Gungahlin Drive and the Barton Highway, which hems in the sprawling 1980s suburbs of Lawson, Kaleen and Giralang. There to the north is Crace and Nicholls, and even further north are Franklin, Palmerston, the suburb of Gunghalin, Harrison, Casey, Ngunnawal, Amaroo and Forde.

These are other-worldly places for the residents of old Canberra, so foreign are the style of houses and the patchy unfinished landscapes of the new estates.

Some people who live in Canberra's original suburbs, with their curved streets planted by Charles Weston, the first horticulturalist charged with foresting the plains, look down upon Gungahlin. Gungahlin is new and neat, many of its trees not yet grown to the point where they fully shade the footpaths or screen out neighbours' houses. Canberra once thumbed its nose at Nappy Valley. But today some of it sneers upon its great northern expanses. Whereas once the great Canberra divide was between north and south, today it is between old and new – inner and outer.

The irony of this in such a staunch Labor town seems profound. For these suburbs represent, consistent with the original Canberra ideal, part of an egalitarian dream: they are big, double-bathroomed houses, sometimes built up to the borders of their blocks, often with dual garages and swimming pools, close to native grasslands, sporting fields, good schools and shops. They are affordable and, in places like Gungahlin and Crace, they also set new standards in energy efficiency – which cannot be said for some of the suburbs of the 1970s, 80s and 90s – or of old Canberra.

I live in the 'inner south'. But I've often been to Gungahlin in winter to stand beside frozen playing fields in misty minus temperatures to watch my son play Australian Rules Football. Sometimes after the half-time siren I've skived off and explored new Canberra. And yes – there are bookshops, fine wine merchants, bars, specialty fashion stores, cafés and restaurants. The people of Gungahlin and Amaroo do not look or dress differently from those of Griffith in the inner south, or Reid and Ainslie in the north. More and more professionals – economists, journalists, information technology specialists and senior public servants – are buying there. Of course, the great outer expanses hosted some of the first white communities in the capital region. The inner 'old' establishment suburbs were a product of much later development that took shape only after the capital was named.

Today, Ginninderra Creek has been tamed by a series of man-made water courses, spillways and drains that snake through suburbia and into manufactured Lake Ginninderra. The creek re-emerges on the other side and culminates in a series of impressive waterfalls on privately held land at the Murrumbidgee across the New South Wales border. The stories of so many of the original settlers like Crace and his driver – who drowned somewhere about where Belconnen stands today – rest deep in a suburbia that many assume has no history.

William Davis raised a cricket team from his property. Ginninderra played other teams drawn from other properties like Duntroon and Tuggeranong, and from Goulburn, Queanbeyan and Braidwood. Davis's matches were always major social as well as sporting events. A brass band often played before the matches began. Evenings of dance and partying followed. Davis was such a cricket enthusiast he instituted a five-and-a-half-day working week so his employees could practise and play on Saturday afternoons. Three local Aboriginal people – Bobby Deumonga, and the Taylor brothers, Johnny and Jimmy – played for Ginninderra. Bobby Deumonga later married Nellie Hamilton. Nellie would later become 'Queen Nellie' after marrying King Billy, who'd come up from the South Coast. She and Billy remained leaders of the local Aboriginal communities. Until her death in 1897, she was outspoken about the dispossession of her people.

She said in 1895:

> I no tink much of your law. You come here and take my land, kill my possum, my kangaroo; leave me starve. Only gib me rotten blanket. Me take calf or sheep, you been shoot me, or put me in jail. You bring your bad sickness 'mong us.

Her succinct and honest summation of the plight of the local Aboriginal people appeared in Gale's book. Nellie's words were originally recounted by Samuel Schumack, another notorious Canberra storyteller.

Part of Schumack's story can also be found in St John's churchyard:

> In memory of Samuel Schumack
> Of Spring Vale Weetangara
> A native of County Cork, Ireland
> Pioneer of this District. Arrived
> 1856 Duntroon. 1850–1946.

Robert Campbell's son George, who'd taken over Duntroon after his father's death, hired Schumack's father Richard as he stood on the deck of the *Bermondsey*, the ship that brought the family to Australia. A few years later, Richard Schumack began working as a shepherd for Davis at Emu Bank, a few miles from the Ginninderra homestead. The Schumacks would later farm their own land at nearby Weetangara.

Samuel Schumack collected stories from the plains for his entire life. Some he wrote down and passed on to his friend Gale, who published them in *The Queanbeyan Age*. Towards the end of his life, Schumack filled a book with all of his recollections. As I sit in the Manuscript Reading Room of the National Library of Australia and struggle to read the brittle yellowed pages of Biro scrawl – barely legible, misspelt and unpunctuated, in the hand of an old, old man who could barely see – so many events take vivid shape.

> You could ride at that time all day and see not a fence ... father made our boots and mother with our sisters help all the clothes for males and females and also for other people stockings were all home knit and father made all the furniture this he did at night and the Saturday afternoons and it was the same right up until mother's death at spring vale in 1873 and up to that sad event we were a happy family and after supper during the winter mother and the girls would be busy with their dress making and John would read to them tales from books and magazines newspapers were scarce at that time ...

Schumack portrays a rugged early life of few comforts in a place of harsh weather, inhabited by escaped convicts, child murderers, bushrangers and other assorted villains.

One of his earliest recollections is of a neighbour, Mrs Kavanagh, being murdered.

' ... her head was found on the river bank a mile from her home with a stone in it and a few hours later her body was discovered I and several other youngsters saw the body taken from the river it was a sad sight ...'

In 1860, as a ten-year-old tending the Davis's

flock, Schumack came across O'Brien, a shepherd from another station. O'Brien, a former convict, threatened to kill the boy. Schumack set his dog onto him and raced home.

Schumack's memory also fixed on 'a sad unsolved mystery in the family in the headstone in the Church of England cemetery'.

He was, I think, probably referring to the 'prophetic' Webb headstone that recorded the death not only of Sarah in childbirth, but also her daughter Betsy Celia.

> ... Betsy Celia ... one evening Celia went to bring in the cows some of them were in sight when she left the house and no trace of this poor child was ever seen or discovered this is one of many unsolved mysteries no doubt this child was a victim to some inhuman brute ...

In 1834 German naturalist Dr John Lhotsky visited the Limestone Plains. He stayed with Ainslie, later recording his observations in *A Journey from Sydney to the Australian Alps.*

Lhotsky was appalled by the living conditions of some convict labourers.

> In this lonely place we were met by a prisoner, belonging to a neighbouring station, who barefooted and covered with rags, reminded me forcibly, that I was in a land of banishment and expiation. I asked him how he came to be so badly off, he replied that the slops were issued very irregularly, and was besides of the very worst description.
>
> He was also all over affected with the Syphilitic disorder, and told me, that many men were in the same situation, without any surgeon at hand. I shook my head, as it appeared to me as if some demon sentenced to perdition was addressing me in this valley of desolation. I had no medicine with me for such cases, but I offered him my good services when returning to Sydney. He declined every offer with a mournful resignation, saying that he should soon be entitled to freedom.

Many who dreamt of earning freedom and establishing homes on their own land would be disappointed. The best they could hope for was the use of a small piece of a master's property to raise a few sheep, a small crop and a family – if they could find a wife.

The land, at five shillings an acre, was too expensive for all but the likes of Campbell, Moore and George Palmer. Palmer, another veteran of the Napoleonic Wars (he fought as a lieutenant in the 1798 Battle of the Nile) established a stock station, Palmerville, at Ginninderra in 1826. Palmer's father John – for many years Commissary of the Colony – arrived in 1788 with Captain Arthur Phillip on the First Fleet ship *Sirius* (his sister, Sophia Palmer, married Robert Campbell in 1801). The Palmers were later granted land at Jerrabomberra. Meanwhile, Thomas Macquoid, the sheriff of the Supreme Court of New South Wales, in 1835 bought a vast parcel of land in the Tuggeranong Valley. Originally known as Waniassa, the station would become Tuggeranong after it was taken over by the Cunningham family in the 1840s. In 1837 Terrence Murray – already an established pastoralist with land at Collector – established his sheep station south of the Molonglo on land known to the Aboriginals as 'Yarrowlumla'. By the time Murray occupied the land its name had been Anglicised to Yarralumla.

The plains, Lhotsky observed, belonged 'by

grant or purchase to a few (although very worthy) landholders'.

'And although five shillings per acre is far too much for primary grants to Emigrants or well behaved freed men, it is far too little for those already possessing large property, who in that way might now purchase entire Dukedoms.'

During early settlement, convicts not required as government labour were assigned to the land-holders. They were often treated very badly and lived harsh existences, as the archival historian Watson noted.

> These men led rude and rough lives, tending the sheep and cattle of their masters, and wanting entirely the disciplinary influences of civilisation … For the first ten years and even in the second decade [of settlement], the district was much disturbed by the depredations of gangs of convicts, who had absconded from the government or from assigned service. These convicts were known as bushrangers, and existed by robbing and plundering isolated settlers.

Watson wrote that the Limestone Plains were 'infested' with bushrangers and that at one stage the situation became so dangerous that a military officer and fifteen men were sent to the area to sort it out. In 1834 the Bushranging Act was renewed. It gave any free person the right to apprehend a stranger who they suspected of being an escaped convict.

But bushranging continued largely unabated for decades, with such notables as Dublin Jack, William Westwood (or 'Jackey Jackey'), Ben Hall and John Tennant evading the law for years. Tennant, a convict who had been assigned to work on J.J. Moore's property, was the 'terror of Argyle' in the late 1820s. Ainslie tracked Tennant down in 1828. He was convicted and jailed.

Some, like 'Waterloo Tom' – who roamed the plains with a knife that he had fashioned from the large, curved blade of a scythe, and attacked shepherds and other settlers for their food and money – were sinister, frightening characters. The threat of flogging, long prison terms, or even the gallows offered little deterrence.

Davis and George Palmer effectively declared war on the bushrangers of the region, vowing if they came across them – especially Hall and his gang – they would shoot on sight. Hall apparently heard about this. Together with his cohorts, Dunn and Gilbert, he set about getting in first. About 1863 Davis caught the coach to Sydney to buy a new revolver-loading rifle. Returning on the afternoon mail coach, he alighted from the cabin at Geary's Gap, a steep hill on the western bank of Lake George, to lighten the horses' load.

Schumack later recounted:

> … he heard throw up your hands or we will scatter your brains and here was Hall and Gilbert and his revolver was taken … there were six women in the coach these were not molested in any way and now Davis was overhauled his fifty guinea watch was taken by Hall who … thanked him for it and Gilbert thanked him for the rifle Well friends Hall said this is the gent that was going to give us hell if we ever came near him what a quiet man he is now … and now Charlott Lydley a passenger on the coach surprised all hands she addressed the Bushrangers in these terms What do ye mean by such conduct as this if ye don't give up this wicked life ye will go to that awful bad place we hear about … when ye die. Not us Dunn said shut up good looking men like us don't go to such bad places only ugly old vixens like you go to such bad places this caused a laugh and Hall and Co made away.

Hall also took Davis's belt.

Police tracked Hall and shot him. He died holding Davis's revolver, wearing his watch and belt.

Palmer's son, George Charles Palmer, quit the family property to become one of those his father detested. He was convicted of murder and hanged in 1869.

Not all escaped convicts became bushrangers.

Some were caught and taken to a convict prison on Moore's land at Acton where they were flogged or put in the stocks. The old prison was demolished in the 1920s when the first buildings of the capital were erected. For years, farmers and builders uncovered leg irons and hand manacles from the earth.

Gale maintained the last official flogging in Canberra happened on Christmas Day in the late 1870s.

Schumack, meanwhile, recounted how offenders were also secured to a tree for flogging outside the court house at Yarralumla from the 1850s. Previously the sentence was carried out while the alleged perpetrator was tied to a great wooden triangle – abandoned after one convict, the hutkeeper Maurice Welsh, somehow capsized it.

> Maurice was being flogged in his agonizing struggle he capsized the triangle and two men were severely injured this did not save Maurice he was then bound to a … tree and got several extra lashes such was his reward for upsetting the triangle … heard some strange stories about his strength and four staples was out in the … tree and many were flogged here after the matter recorded When Dr Murray secured the property [Yarralumla] in the early fifties he had this tree cut down I … saw the stump for the last time in 1910 two staples were in it about a foot from the ground but no grass grew around it.

Another early settler, William Davis Wright, made considerable efforts to communicate with local Aboriginal people.

> When the whites first came to Queanbeyan (probably about 1837) Hongkong was chief of the Kamberra tribe. It was not a very troublesome crowd … From many conversations I had with various members of the tribe, I got to know them and their customs pretty well … Their corroboree ground was at Kamberra, as far as I can gather, the exact spot being near the Canberra Church

> [St John's] ... It served also as their general and best known meeting place. It was an ordinary-sized tribe, between 400 and 500, at the time of the first white settlement.

'Hongkong' was actually OnYong. As Ngambri chief he travelled extensively around the Limestone Plains, even occasionally to Yass and Goulburn.

At least once, OnYong was shot while stealing stock. But ultimately he died in intertribal violence, speared by another Aboriginal, Jimmy the Rover, in a battle over land access. While Jimmy the Rover was from the same Walgalu language group, he was a member of the Ngurmal tribe whose land lay south of the Ngambri's.

Wright, the squire of Lanyon homestead, witnessed OnYong's burial. It was recounted by a number of early historians, but most accurately by Frederick Watson.

> The body was trussed in the knee-elbow position, and the fat about the kidneys was removed. The fat was supposed to possess great virtues, and was distributed to the gins, who carried it in the bags which were hung from their necks. A hole was dug in the ground, at the bottom of which a small

> tunnel was excavated. In this tunnel the body was placed, together with the chief's weapons for use in the next world. The grave was then filled in. Wright records that a settler in later years dug up the skull from this grave and converted it into a sugar basin.

Ngambri descendants believe OnYong was probably their tribe's last full-blood member.

Most inter-racial conflict and violence at the time could be traced, from as early as the late 1820s, to stock theft and the rape by shepherds and convict labourers of native women.

Watson comments: 'The aborigines were naturally peaceful, but when the stock-keepers interfered with their women, they retaliated, and it was not always the guilty parties who suffered.'

Some owners, like Davis Wright, were kind to Aboriginal people. Others made no attempt at civility and treated them with unremitting cruelty – worse than animals. *The Sydney Herald* alluded to this on 31 October 1834, editorialising that the 'indigenes' of the Limestone Plains had been accused of spearing sheep and cattle but that 'this … is likely to be without foundation, it being probable that the same is published with a view to covering some of the delinquencies of the stock-keepers and others in care of their masters' stock'.

The white man's vices and diseases diminished the black population during the 1840s. Samuel Schumack wrote that by the time his family arrived in 1856 the 'tribe of aboriginals numbered about sixty ... A few years later they were reduced to less than a dozen – rum and measles had decimated them.'

This was probably an exaggeration, given the white man's other later observations about the big corroborees and the hunt for migratory bogong moths every year as the weather warmed.

The moths were cooked and eaten as they were caught. The excess insects were pounded into paste and preserved for the leaner, colder months.

A descendant of Sarah Webb recalled how the tribes would meet in the hills and mountains to gather the larvae and cook them on a great flat stone on her family property near the Murrumbidgee at Uriarra.

'You know the big flat rock level with the rest of the yard, out by the stables? Well that is Ura-yarra which means, in the blacks' language, running to the feast,' she told Gale.

> It was the yearly custom of the blacks to assemble from all the neighbouring districts, with their gins and piccaninnies, to some hundreds in number, for the purpose of feasting on the grubs [before they matured into the pupa stage] ... The big flat rock, which was some yards in length and scarcely less in width, was heaped up with dry wood and bark. This was set fire to ... These [grubs] were shaken out from the dilly-bags onto the heated rock and were soon hissing and spluttering, the sign of their being sufficiently cooked ... It was a season of luscious feasting, something so far better than possum and yams, that the ebony skins of the eaters literally shone, and their bodies showed a plumpness quite in contrast with the leanness of normal times.

By the late nineteenth century, the third generation of some of the original settler families was running the major properties.

A resident of Queanbeyan, G.G. Perceval, recalled Duntroon in the 1870s:

> How quaint the little village looked, with the blacksmith's forge, its carpenter's workshop, its brickyard (over by the woolshed), its horse-

> breaker's yard and plant, and other trade and business centres, all conforming to the primitive pattern of the period. The palatial Campbell homestead, known distinguishingly as 'Duntroon' lay off, with an air of aristocratic reserve, a little out of line, surrounded by generous roods of separating space. The quaint old church stood just round the shoulder of the mountain spur, adding the last touch of easy-going dignity. What a picture it all made, set there amid its fringe of scattered farms.

Perceval recalled the homestead was surrounded by trees; one from each country in the world, or so it was said, that was accessible at the time.

> What most of all caught my youthful imagination was a real, living and growing cork tree, the sight and touch of whose bark dispelled at last my lingering skepticism regarding the statement of our old schoolmaster at Queanbeyan as to the source from which the corks for our fishing floats, and incidentally, in their burnt condition, for the blacking of our faces for our occasional nigger entertainments, were derived.
>
> Those premises represented, in Canberra's

> halcyon days, the centre of organization and authority for the brave little community. Miles away, at Woden and Mugga Mugga, were the back stations, where, during the round of the year, the wool grew calmly in the sheep's backs, to be shorn at Woden or Duntroon woolshed.

As a child Perceval watched the shearers at Duntroon – 'strange rough men' he called them – whisper as if in some foreign tongue to the sheep they'd accidentally cut with the shears while the tar boy ran over to seal the wound. And the Chinese cook:

> half terror and half curiosity – a real furious terror when … he was set upon at the prompting of some lads with a mind for a wrong kind of joke, by a drunken black gin, one of the straggling aboriginal community – who, on refusal of her attentions, employed her fists and finger nails, along with 'language' suited to the process.

A visitor in 1872 described the bucolic splendour of the plains when viewed from the northern heights.

> Just at the foot of it [the range] was a pond (or waterhole as they call it here) surrounded with willows, and cattle grazing on fresh grass. On the right was the pretty church with the ivy growing over it, and the new parsonage not far off. In front the plain rolled away right up to the black forests with which all the hills are covered. Here and there, on the plain, are caught sight of a rustic cottage with its bark roof and rough looking sheds attached.

In 1927, the year the provisional Parliament House opened in Canberra, Watson wrote, 'virtually nothing remains to indicate the former existence of the aborigines, the original inhabitants of Canberra, except a few place names'.

This was untrue. There were still many descendants of the original inhabitants living on the Limestone Plains, although few, if any, would have been 'pure blood'. But it suited the settler narrative that the blacks had, sadly, all died off or just wandered away.

Some claimed they were gone well before the turn of the twentieth century. Lhotsky, for example, wrote in 1834 after his visit that 'they are no more'.

That's not quite true, as the appearance of

Jimmy Clements – 'King Billy' – and his mate John Noble at the opening of federal Parliament in May 1927 would attest. Clements was a Wuradjuri man from the south-west, out near Gundagai. But he was well known also, particularly towards the end of his life, around the Limestone Plains. Like so many of the Aboriginal 'kings' he was really just a king to the whites, who picked tribal leaders they felt they could communicate with and gave them copper breast plates, bearing their names, to wear around their necks.

Having walked overland from Gundagai with Noble, he presented a shabby sight at the opening of Parliament. He wanted to meet the officiating Duke and Duchess of York. The police shooed him away. But some of the locals protested and he was presented to them.

Notorious for having met the royals, Clements died a few months later, as reported by the papers. One story in *The Barrier Miner* of 31 August 1927 typically said he belonged to the last of the 'tribe of aborigines who roamed the plains and hills of Canberra long before the Federal Capital was dreamed of', even though he belonged to a different tribe altogether.

Some of the older settlers across the Limestone

Plains who knew Jimmy thought that the capital should commemorate him with a stone or perhaps a bronze statue.

The politicians dismissed the idea. At a dinner in his electorate the member for Ballarat, David McGrath, said in 1928 to great laughter: 'If I had my way on this matter I would give Canberra to King Billy and his tribe.'

McGrath had played shrewdly to the already extant anti-Canberra sentiment of the country beyond the room he was addressing.

They buried King Billy in an unmarked grave on the edge of Queanbeyan Cemetery, just beyond the consecrated ground; a black man could not be put to rest in blessed earth.

There would be no stone, no bronze statue for Jimmy Clements or any other black man.

There would be no place for that among the monuments that newly federated Australia would build in honour of itself.

Monuments in the Grass

Like most who live here, I have my place, a piece of urban bush where I lose myself and find myself. It's not actually mine. The great egalitarian ideal that some of the dreamers had for Canberra never fully materialised – but it is symbolised by the access that all have to the best views along the ridges, hills and mountains that corral the Limestone Plains.

You can be a multimillionaire here. But you still can't buy the heights. They are reserved for the dog walkers, the runners and the twitchers.

My place is Red Hill. When the dog and I get to the top we stop and look both ways across the range: north across the bones of the Griffins' plan, and south over Woden and into Tuggeranong Valley.

In summer we'll sit and wait in the hope of seeing the pair of eagles who've nested high in one of the Ngambri's sacred gums. We'll sit and watch them for an hour. The dog's snout will rise and roll as her eyes trace, when she finally focuses, the great birds above us as they effortlessly twirl and dance, moon-walking on the updraughts.

Today, the dog whinnies and hesitates. I try to coax her along the narrow track of crunching gravel that is hedged on each side by waist-height dried grass and weed. But she shifts her considerable weight into her haunches and clenches her muscles, immovably locking herself to the track. Not a vocal dog, she surprises me by growling softly. Then a brown snake – no longer or thicker than a pencil but armed with sufficient venom to kill a giraffe – whips across our path. The dog, neurotic, sweet and antsy and with such bad eyesight that she seems to think that kangaroos, too, are dogs, has smelt the snake well before I've sensed it. It's the first one I've seen this year, which everyone reckons is going to be a shocker for snakes.

I know what to do when encountering a snake: stay perfectly still, keep the dog away and under no circumstances – none! – strike it with the stick that I always carry for just such occasions.

Snake stories are legion here.

Whenever we're in the vet's waiting room I ask, 'Many snakes so far?', knowing I'll elicit at least one good snake story.

I picked up a great tale from another pet owner about a man who'd been running up on the hill with his Jack Russell when they encountered an unusually aggressive, well-fed tiger, fat with frogs and mice. The dog and snake struck at the same time. The bare-chested man ran into the vet with a bundle in his T-shirt and rolled it onto the gurney. The snake's head was secured in the dog's teeth, the snake coiled around its body. Both were alive and in an embrace of mutually assured destruction. The vet euthanised the snake. He then sedated the dog so that its Araldite jaws could be prised from the snake.

It might be a true story. It might be based on any number of stories. It doesn't matter. Snakes are about. Every year they bite people and dogs.

It is the beginning of summer. I happened to be listening to local radio when a listener rang to say a red-belly black snack had become trapped in the underground car park at Parliament House.

I fear snakes. But recently I've wondered if I've perhaps lived here too long, because I have stopped consciously looking out for snakes which, over the years, I've seen in my garden and in the bush cutting at the top of my street.

An American military family once lived opposite

us. The wife was paranoid about snakes, just as she was always full of wonder at the kangaroos that make their way from the bushy heights into Canberra's suburban streets to drink from the swimming pools. We sometimes pass 'roos while driving. We see their decomposing carcasses on the verges. They cause fatal accidents. And they are a part of our lives.

My favourite story from the veterinary frontline involves the eagles. I heard it from a young Irish locum, so it must be true – unless, of course, mindful of my appetite for dog stories, he just made it up.

'Any snake bites?' I asked.

'Aye – couple. But did you hear about the eagles? Swooped down and took off the lady's wee dog, a Chihuahua it was. She had it off lead and your eagle took it up and dropped it. That's the way an eagle kills its prey. Must have taken it for a rabbit or more likely a rat.' It survived.

That is a dog story.

Only to the visiting outsider does the convergence of the natural and the urban seem anomalous. Canberra is intelligent and it is urbane. It is highly educated and wealthy. It has the best roads in the country and the roomiest, most comfortable and perhaps, on balance, some of the least aesthetic houses on the continent. But it is also surrounded by the Australian bush. The animals and birds, like the bushfires and floods that threaten us cyclically, and like the bogong moths that are lured each spring by the death-glow of our houselights, remind us of our physical vulnerability.

On Wednesday, 4 September 1940, the British-born feminist and artist Eilean Giblin, having arrived in Canberra a few days earlier, wrote in her diary about the consuming silence of the wartime city.

> I am getting used to the silence of Canberra, and am no longer expecting to hear Melbourne trams. A car passes occasionally and the voices of children come to one now and then; but generally there may be only the clucking of hens, ours, or our neighbours, or the birds, sparrows … and in the late afternoon several kookaburras calling and laughing from the telegraph poles at the back of the garden.

Giblin was writing about Forrest, where she lived with her husband – adventurer, warrior and Labor political economist Lyndhurst Falkiner Giblin.

When I walk through the hills I tell myself

that I'm searching for peace and quiet. But I'm really seeking the opposite. My street is as quiet as an undertaker's parlour. On some days I don't see anyone when I look onto the street from my desk. What I am really seeking when I walk up and along my ridge is a connection with the world. I love the sounds of the wind and the birds – and of the traffic on Hindmarsh Drive.

It's true that London is a city of villages that all lead to the city, with its sectors for banking and finance, politics, entertainment, retail shopping and, until the mid-1980s, media.

Canberra is a city of suburban strip shops that lead to shopping centres in malls that lead to plazas. For decades Canberra life has played itself out in the strip shops that serve most suburbs. The small suburban centres are where you'll find the best bars, restaurants, music venues, bookshops, cafés and clothing stores. Visitors who go to Civic in search of the city's 'life' miss the point and leave disappointed. Canberra does not readily disclose itself.

Robyn Archer, the creative director of the capital's centenary festivities, Canberra100, pointed out to me a recent piece in a small-circulation Australian magazine written by an academic who works locally but lives across the border in New South Wales. It was the usual anti-Canberra rant (cold in winter, baking in summer, public servants, socially isolated, no spontaneity – and so on and on) that culminated in the proposition that to eat well at a restaurant if you live here, you might need to drive to Griffith or Sydney.

Which reminds me of a chapter about Canberra in a book by Bill Bryson. He came to Canberra and predictably discovered some roundabouts, and even a motorist who appeared lost on one (looking for his house; sure!), couldn't find a restaurant or a decent pub, explored the city entirely on foot (apparently) and chose to stay at the Rex Hotel on Northbourne Avenue – in a well-known zone of lifelessness. (Incidentally, the Rex, where Lyndon Johnson stayed in the 60s, is being restored to its former elegance. Bryson ought to have stayed there in the 70s, because that's the last time it rocked. Or he could have made a slight effort and found one of the many boutique hotels near a good restaurant. But then, he'd have to go to Sydney or even Griffith for that, wouldn't he?)

Bryson's Canberra chapter was a laugh. Cheap.

But yes, a laugh. Not to mention perfectly pitched at Australia's prejudices and ignorance about Canberra.

Bryson's book was published a decade ago. But some people who live here are still seething with anger about it. At a speech I gave on my writing about Canberra, a woman mentioned Bryson's effort. She told me she still wanted to give him a piece of her mind.

I told her I thought it was just lazy humour – don't worry.

I said: 'At least he made the effort to come here, which is more than the critics he's pandering to. And besides Canberra can seem dead unless you know where to go – it's a city that reveals itself to you slowly. You have to work at it.'

'That's not the point,' she said. 'It's just that these sort of attacks make us feel worthless.'

As Canberra turns one hundred, a new wave of development is reshaping the inner city – the very places around Civic, Acton, the Kingston Foreshore and Causeway and Constitution Avenue that Griffin had envisaged would be alive with the type of residential, entertainment and retail hustle and bustle that characterises urban life. I've long considered Northbourne Avenue – its dingy northern reach implanting road visitors from Sydney and Melbourne with a depressing vista of outer Vilnius minus the pollution – an ugly urban disgrace.

But as the city's population moves towards 400 000, the 'urban infill' plan would bring Northbourne to life with attractive, architect-designed apartments that incorporate retail, entertainment and recreation. Kingston is already being similarly developed, while newly built parts of 'New Acton' around the Diamant Hotel have corners and pockets – cafés, food retailers, bars, apartments – that define a genuine inner city. The problem is that some of the buildings have been built too high for those who believe the city's urban integrity must always rest with the sight-line of mountain and water. Such purists complain, for example, that some buildings at New Acton, which I love, impede the view of Black Mountain, the Brindabellas and the lake from the important axis point of City Hill at the end of Commonwealth Avenue.

As Allan Hawke, who undertook an extensive inquiry into Canberra's development in 2011, said to me: 'There are 350 000 people in Canberra and there are 350 000 town planners, because everybody has got an opinion about how it ought to be done.'

In his respected book that incisively plots the capital's evolution, *Canberra Following Griffin: A Design History of Australia's National Capital*, the former head of Canberra's National Capital Development Commission, Paul Reid, considers the greatest national misconception about this place is that it's the city of Walter Griffin.

> Today Canberra's citizens proudly claim Griffin as the designer of their city. They usually invoke his name to justify any particular interpretation of the plan they favour at the time. The impression given is that modern Canberra is Griffin's city, with a few changes necessitated by modern life, of which he would have approved. In fact the vitality of Griffin's proposed urban terraces and monuments has been replaced by quiet suburbs on a serene landscape.

Those who live here will attest to Canberra's quietness and serenity. But only to first-time visitors, or residents who aren't trying, are quietness and serenity synonyms for benign dullness. Beyond the two parliament buildings and the national institutions such as the National Library of Australia, the National Archives, the National Museum and the Australian War Memorial, Canberra's gems (cassoulet worthy of Carcassonne in Civic; ethnic Indian in Pearce to rival Edgeware Road; galleries in Fyshwick, Deakin and Griffith to match Paddington's; eclectic, reader-friendly bookshops worthy of Charing Cross Road in Braddon, Manuka, Mawson and Curtin; stunning produce at the Mitchell farmer's market) largely remain secreted in unlikely suburban shopping strips and even its industrial parks. That is central to its charm and wonder. If Reid is, as I think, correct, then such charm and wonder has emerged almost in spite of the countless compromises that a century of urban growth and incessant redesign has imposed on Griffin's original plan and the federation dream underpinning it.

To appreciate this we need to go back to the notion of an Australian capital that accompanied federation and to understand the force that has shaped Canberra unlike any other Australian city.

Politics.

From its very conception, the notional Australian capital had been the preserve of politicians. Their decisions dictated its location, it design and its evolution from the beginning – even though the publicly elected officials would move on and the city would fight for and win permanence.

By the late 1890s, Australia's economy was dependent on the bush – 'the sheep's back'. But most people lived in the colonies' big rural towns and cities.

The Limestone Plains sent wool to Sydney and Melbourne. By then, thanks to William James Farrer, the region was becoming a leading wheat producer too. Farrer was a man of eclectic interests and talents, including what he saw as scientific garderning. At Lambrigg on the west bank of the Murrumbidgee just upstream of Point Hutt Crossing (close to the territory border) Farrer experimented with hybrid wheat that he designed specifically to avoid the 'rust' that ruined so many colonial crops.

His work made possible Australia's wheat industry. In the same part of Australia where Farrer experimented, the CSIRO continues his work at the vanguard of agricultural research.

By this time, the big estates were delineated with

fences. Fencing dramatically reduced the number of labourers required to tend stock. Basic mechanical farming methods had been introduced, and those once employed as shepherds and harvesters became jobless. They roamed the district looking for work or handouts. Charity was scarce. Some went bush to live off the land and in camps with Aboriginal people. Dotted around the big English-style estates were smaller, marginally viable family farms. Subsistence was tenuous.

Rain patterns were erratic. Frederick Watson described the climate's impact on the waters of Lake George.

> Lake George had been quite dry in the years 1838 and 1839, and again from 1846 to 1850. In the year 1852 … the lake filled up again. In the 'seventies it shrank to a morass ten miles long and two miles wide. In 1881 it began to fill up again; but, in 1885, there was again a severe drought. This was followed by a few years of good seasons, and then by a drought in the nineties. During a hundred years the fluctuations in Lake George have been between the two extremes of a magnificent lake about fifteen miles long and five miles broad, with a depth of twenty four feet, and

of a dry expanse of country with stock grazing on the bed of the lake.

By federation, the once perfectly managed plains were degraded, courtesy of eight decades of running stock. And there was a new menace – rabbits. There were tens of thousands of them. They destroyed vast tracts of cropland and halved the availability of grazing land.

Coupled with the erratic rain patterns, rabbits made farming the plains economically parlous, even for the big landholders.

The plains' smaller farmers had no special interest in federation beyond its potential impact on the market prices of their stock, wool and grain – and the access to new markets after the removal of colonial tariffs.

Wealthier landowners with access to travel and literature were more likely to understand the broader ideals that underpinned colonial federation, without which an Australian capital – and Canberra – would not have happened.

In the two decades to 1899 Australia hosted eight 'international exhibitions' that aspired, in the vein of England's Great Exhibition at Crystal Palace in 1851, to showcase the best of local culture, industry and architecture. Visitors to any of those exhibitions could only have left optimistic that the colonies had transcended the convict past and moved to a new strata of enlightened, democratised civilisation.

Despite rivalries that characterised relations between Mother New South Wales and the newer colony of Victoria, the well-attended exhibitions in Sydney and Melbourne of 1879 and 1880 were the focus of united pride. Potential economic reforms, such as tariff removal, national co-ordination of post, rail gauge standardisation and eventually banking, shaped forceful arguments that motivated the public towards embracing federation. Just as important, the early 'national' pride engendered by the exhibitions underpinned a basic federal ideal: together we colonies could make a better, brighter, more egalitarian and prosperous nation.

Sir Henry Parkes, the most passionate and influential colonial proponent of federation, died in 1896, his dream close but unrealised. It was for others like George Reid, Edmund Barton, Alfred Deakin, Chris Watson and John Forrest to realise.

As the colonial conventions of 1897–98 thrashed out a future Australian Constitution, parochialism characterised debate about the location of federal Parliament. The idealism at federation's heart also underpinned the notion of a national capital – if not for all of the less than altruistic politicians, than at least as far as some of Australia's foremost planners, engineers and architects were concerned. Ultimately, political expediency dictated that the Constitution specify the capital be built in New South Wales (the New South Wales premier, George Reid, could not otherwise get the support at a second referendum in 1899 of his colony's self-imposed requisite 80 000 voters).

Section 125 of the Constitution also dictated that the capital would be at least one hundred miles from Sydney and should be at least one hundred square miles in size. It also determined that Parliament would sit in Melbourne until the new seat of government was determined.

In negotiating Section 125, Reid might have thought he'd come away with a good deal. But he had actually guaranteed Sydney could never become the national capital or host federal Parliament. It meant that Melbourne would do so indefinitely, effectively making it de facto capital.

Most New South Wales politicians beyond Sydney's hundred-mile radius argued for their electorates to host the capital. Why not? The wily Parkes first espoused the perfection of his town, Albury, in the 1850s, when federation was still his pipedream.

In 1899 William Lyne became premier of New South Wales. He swiftly appointed a royal commissioner, Alexander Oliver, 'to make full inquiries as to the suitability for the seat of government of the Commonwealth of Australia of such tracts or areas as you might be invited to consider'.

Oliver advertised for submissions. He received proposals for forty-five sites, visited twenty-three and held public inquiries in fourteen.

As royal commissioner, Oliver brought a commendable sense of irony and cynicism to his task. He later wrote:

> In the course of my inspections nothing struck me as more remarkable than the unswerving loyalty of the witnesses to their climates. No matter what the day temperature might be, the nights were always cool, and if the districts rejoiced in a steady sequence of seasonable frosts … Snow never lay more than a few hours on the ground … Where such enclosures as cemeteries existed, I was assured that nine-tenths of the occupants

> had been 'undesirables' who came to the township as a last resource. Medical men came, looked, and went away disheartened; or if they stayed, became poultry farmers, or cultivated an orchard or a vineyard. An immense pumpkin chased me round several sites. It was the silent witness for climate as well as soil, and not being liable to cross-examination, did yeoman's service. Finally, there was the hale old man past eighty, and the cured consumptive, all bearing eloquent testimony to the matchless salubrity of their site.

Oliver didn't feel confined to the minimum hundred square miles for the capital territory. He grouped potential sites into three districts – the western, the south-western and the southern. He then commended highly one site in each: Orange (or Canobolas), Yass and Bombala–Eden.

Oliver was a proponent of the 'cold climate' school of thought – something of a nod to the philosophies of eugenics whereby people were thought to function more efficiently in a bracing climate.

'The federal territory should have an invigorating climate ... both the sanatorium and the nerve centre of the nation,' he wrote. In Canberra, Oliver certainly won an invigorating climate. Mornings here of minus six and seven I've found more challenging than any that three London winters could offer. The nerve centre? Politically, yes. The sanatorium? Never. Well, the lifestyle is excellent.

Oliver's recommendations on the location of the capital were made to the New South Wales Legislative Assembly in late October 1900.

From the south-western group, Oliver recommended Yass on the basis of its temperate climate, its distance from both Sydney and Melbourne, its potential for expansion for a bigger capital territory and the comparative affordability of the requisite land. He proposed that the Yass site should be extended east so that it incorporated Lake George (already crown land and, therefore, effectively free to be used for the new territory) and to the south as far as Queanbeyan. This recommended 950 square mile site almost as an afterthought included, at its far south-eastern corner, the sleepy Parish of Canberra.

His pick of the southern sites was the twin-capital region of Bombala on the eastern slopes of the Snowy Mountains, and the idyllic nearby whaling port of Eden. This became the site he favoured most of all. 'It was the choice,' wrote

Roger Pegrum in his authoritative book, *The Bush Capital: How Australia Chose Canberra as its Federal City*, 'of an outdoors man with a love of the sea, but Oliver must have known that none of its qualities would be attractive to those in power in Sydney.'

How those of us who grew up on the eastern coastal plains sometimes wish Bombala–Eden had prevailed.

Canberra's summer can be stifling. But a mountain breeze inevitably brings relief on all but a few evenings a year. But how frequently I have fantasised after leaving Parliament House and stepping into the furnace outside, of grabbing my board and catching a wave.

Instead we have to drive to the New South Wales South Coast, down Brown Mountain to Bermagui, or risk the treacherous Kings Highway down the Clyde, past 'Pooh Corner' (ask any Canberran) to Batemans Bay. Then it's right on the Pacific Highway for Broulee, Moruya and Congo, left towards Jervis Bay for Durras, Pebbly Beach, Bawley Point and Mollymook.

During that lazy, hazy glorious six weeks when

the Parliament has risen and the public service is reduced to a skeleton, Canberra wears thongs and boardies.

That's when the main streets of these seaside villages are lined with cars bearing blue-and-white number plates, mostly beginning with Y. Y for 'Yogi', which is what the local boardriders sometimes call those of us with our pale tentative sea legs, who paddle uncertainly into the perfect breaks on our shiny newly waxed Malibus from 20 December to 31 January. 'Yogis'.

But there's none of the aggro that you get at Manly or Maroubra, Cottesloe or Bell's when the 'burbs converge on the line-up. Canberra owns and leases many of the houses and helps float the local South Coast economies. We leave in time for the school year, taking our Y-plated cars and our coffee-makers and box sets of *The West Wing* with us, and we return but briefly during the year to mow the buffalo grass and empty the septic. It's a wonderful harmony.

And Bombala? Cold for functional efficiency – yes. But also just a stone's throw from Thredbo and Perisher. Currently we have to drive two hours across the harsh monotone beauty of the Monaro to get to the best skifields in the country.

Second-generation Canberra people grow up skiing those runs. Canberra tells its skiers when to make the effort to leave home in the frosty pre-dawn to make first lifts. Rain and minus five overnight probably means fresh powder at Perisher's Zali's, Olympic and The Chute, and that the glorious snow gum-lined trails and traverses are linking Guthega and Blue Cow and the Front Valley. If you look out your office window in Barton, Russell, Parliament or Woden at white-capped Brindabellas, you'll know the Supertrail is covered from Kosciuszko's peak and that High Noon and Cannonball will be pristine in the morning before the slush. Canberra has always felt an affinity with those small communities in the Snowies. Our earliest skiers were the European tradies – Swiss, Germans, Italians, Poles and Austrians – who moved here to build the city, when Australia finally got around to it, after knocking together the Snowy Mountains Scheme which was, until the 'new' Parliament House opened on Capital Hill in 1988, the most expensive infrastructure project Australia had seen. They built their rustic lodges at Thredbo, Perisher and Jindabyne. They skied hard, played guitars and sang foreign songs and drank their schnapps – blazing an *après* trail whose precedent is enthusiastically upheld today.

Thredbo, especially, had long been a part of Canberra's fabric. Thredbo in winter often seems like a small Canberra enclave. Canberra people – who live with minus mornings, more than half a kilometre above sea level, surrounded by snowy peaks – feel themselves to be mountain people too.

On 27 April 1901 in Melbourne, Australia finally won its Commonwealth Parliament.

But it still had no permanent capital.

The politicians initially cared little. King O'Malley, a man as enigmatic as he was idiosyncratic, was a notable exception. O'Malley claimed to be Canadian-born. But he was most likely American – a self-purported one-time fundamentalist preacher with the 'Redskin Church of the Cayuse Nation', and an alleged crook who'd fled creditors when he came to Australia in 1888 as an insurance salesman.

So eager was he to shroud himself in mystery, the flamboyantly dressed O'Malley even lied about his age, saying he was born on 4 July – American Independence Day – rather than his likely birthday, 2 July.

O'Malley wove an elaborate tale about his coming to Australia: his first wife, an organist in his flock, died of consumption; O'Malley, suffering the same complaint, caught a freighter to Australia and disembarked in far north Queensland; having wandered the beach and found a cave, a courteous Aboriginal man saved him from drowning and cured his consumption by feeding him purple berries.

Ever contradictory, O'Malley waged a life-long campaign against alcohol, while priding himself as a socially progressive libertarian. His abhorrence of 'stagger juice' manifested itself in prohibition, assiduously ignored, in the eventual Federal Capital Territory (as the ACT was first known). O'Malley, twice minister for Home Affairs – the portfolio charged with establishing a capital – arguably had more to do with driving the Canberra project than any other single member of Parliament.

O'Malley belonged to the 'all publicity is good publicity' school of politician. He assiduously clipped the many newspaper articles about him as an MP – first as a Tasmanian independent and later for Labor.

In the opening months of the Parliament the major newspapers variously labelled him a 'clown', a 'non-entity' and the 'embodiment of vulgar display'.

'A poseur every waking moment of his life, theatrical to his finger tips, in both speech and dress, a weak imitator of the spread-eagle orators of the United States,' said *The Age*.

O'Malley would spend his life in public repelling allegations about his past (most of which were true) and simultaneously promoting and defending the colourful reputation he had confected.

Charles Studdy Daley, a senior public servant in the Department of Home Affairs under O'Malley, and who later became the administrator of Canberra, railed against O'Malley, once saying he was unsuitable as a minister and as a 'custodian of this country's traditions'. Even after O'Malley's death in 1953, Daley continued to argue that O'Malley was utterly unworthy of having a Canberra suburb named after him. (But today the suburb of O'Malley stands as defiantly as the man whose name it bears, overlooking the beautiful Woden Valley. With several very notable and highly visible exceptions, it hosts some of Canberra's more architecturally attractive and enviro-friendly homes and diplomatic missions.)

The very attachment of the O'Malley name to

the proposed capital could only guarantee controversy.

While political debate centred on where the capital should be, O'Malley – who recommended the eventual site's freehold should remain with the Commonwealth – enlivened debate by prescribing the aspirations Parliament should have for the capital.

> ... we ought to add all possible attractions to our federal city, by selecting a soil of unsurpassed richness with a fascinating, undulating beauty of surface, in a locality with health-generating climate capable of nurturing a sympathetic and noble-minded people worthy to be the central pivot of this southern empire of Australia.

Non-politicians tried to enlighten discourse with discussion on what – as opposed to merely where – the capital should be. The first meeting of the Congress of Engineers, Architects, Surveyors and Others Interested in Building the Federal Capital of Australia 1901, was deliberately held to coincide with the first session of federal Parliament.

Architect George Sydney Jones recommended to the conference that the symbolism of the capital should aim to be uniquely Australian rather than imperial.

> Let us … not slavishly copy the art of past dead centuries … it is possible to create Architecture, which, while possessing the best of the characteristics of … the great ages of the art, shall reflect also the best, in thought and spirit, which in so comparatively short a time has made us what we are.

The front of the Congress handbook featured a painting by the architect Charles Coulter of an ideal capital city built on Lake George. It seems totally at odds with George Jones's proposition. The painting, held by the National Library, is an utterly extravagant – almost out-of-this-world – imagining, of pompous spires, domes, columns and balustrades, and monolithic public buildings. It is lifeless except for a few nymph-like statues and intimidated, misplaced looking women and children.

The congressmen seemed on a track to somewhere special. But this painting hardly embodied it.

Seven more years of state and federal inquiries, political jockeying and site battles followed before the final location for the capital was chosen. During this time the potential list of sites as recommended, often separately, by the New South Wales and Commonwealth governments, contracted and expanded to include, among others, Tumut, Lyndhurst, Delegate, Gadara, Albury and Dalgety. In 1902 members and senators participated in the now infamous inspection expeditions of shortlisted potential locations.

We're off – it is a special train
For Capitals we're looking
For many days, through
Devious ways
And variegated cooking
Each hill and dale, each stream and lake
Seems all the more alluring,
When sandwiches and bottled ale
Alleviate our touring

This 1902 verse from *Table Talk* journal indicates, perhaps, some of the public cynicism surrounding the tour.

The touring MPs were inevitably shadowed by a legion of journalists, eager at the prospect of watching their elected representatives endure strenuous conditions as they criss-crossed New South Wales by train, carriage and car. Oliver's preferred site, Bombala, fared badly. It was icy cold, and a howling wind blew all day. A local policeman said, 'I declare to God this is the warmest winter I have known.' Meanwhile, one MP described Dalgety, on the Snowy River in the far south-east of the state, as a 'frozen waste where the half-dozen houses seem to have been washed up and left on the bank during a flood'. Dalgety left a permanent impression on senators who'd swum in the Snowy River. Even in summer the ice-fed Snowy is not to be entered lightly. Perhaps the most famous tour photograph depicts half a dozen of them bathing in the river. Two are engaged in a mock fistfight – a gesture for the camera symbolising their disagreement over sites. (Billy Hughes, the future prime minister, took a dip in the Snowy during the tour by lower house members, describing it as 'liquid ice' and later saying he had 'never been the same man since'.)

Most were relieved to return to the heated train at Cooma. Many are said to have stayed in bed the next morning, thereby missing a tour of the Limestone Plains. They moved quickly on to Lake George, providing another enduring photographic image. The panoramic photograph shows the parliamentarians standing in the middle of the empty, parched lakebed close to a dead tree, the horizon washed out by a pall of dust. It was impossible to reconcile with Coulter's dream of an imposing European capital reflecting off the vast baby blue surface of Lake George. Yass, visited later that day, was suffocating in red dust as the MPs made their inspection. Such hastily formed impressions were, in retrospect, most unfair. When the rains have been abundant, especially in spring, the Yass Valley's blanket of pasture and wildflower is an uplifting sight. And passers-by have always found Lake George captivating – and alluring.

For weeks, heavy rain has been flooding most of New South Wales and the territory. The earth of Red Hill, where exposed between trees and grass, glistens a delicious bloody burgundy, like the watercolour in which my little girl renders her tomatoes. The crevices that run with gravity from the crown of my hill, the age-furrows on its old man's face, are swiftly flowing with a dozen crystal-clear streams.

I walk up and let the dog off. She bounds back down and finds the deepest temporary creek. From where I stand up here she looks like a giant otter/black fur seal hybrid. Only her conical snout, her sturdy rump and the tip of her outstretched tail are visible.

She galumphs out of the creek and does the canine Twist, conjuring a glittering miasma – a doggy halo – that catches the harsh sunlight. Then she bolts towards me with her tongue dangling and tail swaying, exuberantly celebrating this day's splendour for both of us. Steam rises from her back.

I look across the plains. Charles Weston's urban forest is almost alarmingly verdant from all that moisture, glowing in parts an almost tree frog green. The tree carpet is tinged with rust in subtle deference to the calendar's new season. So, too, I noticed this morning, is the dogwood tree in my front yard, planted half a century ago by a former ambassador to Washington as a reminder of another artificial capital a hemisphere away.

I know where I need to go in order to fully survey the rejuvenation of the rains. I heard on radio this morning that Lake George has water for the first time in years.

I drive out to the Federal Highway, going around the airport, behind Mount Ainslie and Mount Majura, and past a couple of wineries and farmlets. (When I first arrived, 'Canberra winery' was an oxymoron; today local vineyards produce some of the country's finest wines.)

I drive over the rise to see a thin, mirage-like sheen across the green pan of Lake George. We in Canberra have our official, artificial lakes. But this is the lake that really captivates our imaginations just as it did those of Aboriginal people, the explorers and the early settlers. Everyone knows the lake's mysteries and myths, of the ghosts that lurk around it on misty winter evenings, of the stock and the many people it has supposedly swallowed.

I pull into one of the lookouts. Dozens of other cars, most Canberra-plated, have done the same thing. Their occupants survey the lake with binoculars or photograph it. Under a heavy band of low cloud the surface of the lake is a disappointing dull battleship grey. But when the cloud shifts the lake dances with refracting colour and brilliantly mirrors radiant cloud and vivid blue sky. The easy hills behind the Bungendore shore hold aloft their sculpted wind turbines, emblems of the ongoing political argument about sustainable progress around here. The great white blades cartwheel their reflections across the lake.

It's hard to imagine the lake as malevolent. But the pioneers gathered endless stories about fine days turning ugly, of dramatic rises in water levels, of treacherous currents, undertows and lightning squalls.

I drive closer to the lakebed where a low copse of yellowing poplars rustles, detecting a breeze that I can't.

It's easy to miss the memorial at first, standing unpretentiously there next to a rubbish bin – a simple bronze plaque on a small boulder of granite.

> THIS MEMORIAL IS DEDICATED TO THE MEMORY OF THE LYNCH FAMILY
>
> Christine Agnes Lynch Aged 5 years
> Brenda Ann Lynch Aged 12 years
> Ethel Hope Lynch Aged 33 years
> John Leslie Lynch Aged 38 years
> and
> Raylee Monica Koppman Aged 12 years
> Lost in a boating accident on Lake George
> 12th January 1958
> 'Now safe in God's care'

The Lynches, a public service family from Queanbeyan, planned the day on Lake George as a birthday celebration for five-year-old Christine. But their twelve-foot skiff capsized, killing the parents, their two daughters and their cousin, Monica. Thirteen-year-old Barry Lynch, holidaying at Numeralla, was orphaned.

'Queanbeyan has not forgotten about this accident,' he told *The Queanbeyan Age* fifty years later.

THE MPs returned from their 1902 three-week tour exhausted but convinced that none of the sites they'd visited bore much resemblance to the way they had been previously described.

In 1903 a royal commission effectively recommended the capital be built around Albury–Tumut. But later that same year the Senate determined that it should be Bombala. The bill proposing Bombala sat in the lower house at the end of the parliamentary session. It died when Parliament was prorogued for a December 1903 federal election, the first at which Australian women voted.

Debate continued through the next Parliament,

the next and even the next when Alfred Deakin, prime minister for the second time, prorogued sitting for five months so he could visit London officially.

In 1907 John Forrest, the former Western Australian premier and by that stage one of the few surviving founding fathers of federation, became acting prime minister. As a young man Forrest had been a surveyor and an explorer of the Western Australian interior – experience he put to immediate use as acting prime minister, by exploring Canberra.

Forrest re-endorsed Dalgety (which federal Parliament had chosen as the seat of government in a parliamentary bill that had lapsed in late 1904), saying Canberra had 'nothing of particular importance in either scenery or great natural features … there are no rising knolls for public edifices … the site is not visible till you get near it, while the view from it is not commanding'.

Enter the ageing John Gale, who enjoyed greater political influence than any resident of the Canberra region.

On a prominent corner in Queanbeyan's main street, just outside the courthouse, stands a life-sized statue that was fashioned in 2001 by the

Melbourne sculptor Peter Corlett. It depicts an old man. He is short. But he stands with his back and his shoulders straight. He has a shiny pate but plenty of wavy hair at the temples and a luxuriant beard and moustache. He looks slightly off to his left, more quizzical than intense. He holds a hat in one hand and a rolled-up newspaper – *The Queanbeyan Age* – in the other.

The gold letters on the base of the statue read:

THE FATHER OF CANBERRA
JOHN GALE
1831–1929

The statue makes a bold claim – a parochial assertion at the heart of the century-old contest of supremacy (of lifestyle, of pubs, of water quality, of cafés, of football and all other sport, of 'heart' – of just about anything, really) between Canberra and Queanbeyan. It is an open-and-shut statement, a lay down misere, that says to Canberra, 'Don't even bother arguing about who's the best because we made you.' Queanbeyan delights in the claim that one of its own was responsible for finally getting the wretched politicians to pick Canberra.

On 24 July 1907 Gale delivered a speech to

hundreds in Queanbeyan titled *Dalgety or Canberra: Which?* in which he debunked Forrest's Dalgety proposal. It was an eloquent dissertation in which he factually and rhetorically tore apart Forrest's nine-point argument which covered the proximity of Canberra to Sydney, its water supply, climate, topography, rail linkages, water frontage (the chief engineer advised Gale, presciently, that an artificial lake could easily be made close to the Canberra capital site) and the availability of commanding sites for public buildings.

Gale's speech was sent to every state and federal parliamentarian.

Sure enough, by mid-1908 Parliament was backing Canberra. Thanks to Gale, George Reid (prime minister from August 1904 to August 1905) was on side. So, too, was Chris Watson. In the end, even Forrest, ardent Dalgety man, came around.

Sections of the city press, including *The Bulletin*, had run series after series of deliberately biased anti-Canberra stories, comparing it as a barren, dry, windswept, intemperate and infertile wasteland to the Eden-like Dalgety. In the ninth ballot on 8 October 1908 federal Parliament voted thirty-nine to thirty-three to establish the national capital in the Yass–Canberra region.

The next month, the Senate, after another failed push for Dalgety, finally supported Yass–Canberra. But then Deakin's government fell apart. Andrew Fisher became Labor's second prime minister. He appointed Hugh Mahon as Home Affairs minister with an instruction to finalise the capital issue. On 14 December 1908 the bill naming Yass–Canberra as the site of the capital became law. It specified that the capital territory should be at least 900 miles square and should have 'access to the sea'.

New South Wales would eventually hand over 28 square miles of the most picturesque land on the South Coast at Jervis Bay to be used as a port and naval base. Originally it was envisaged that a railway would link Jervis Bay to the rest of the new territory. But that, like so many other plans for the capital, quickly evaporated.

Fisher moved quickly to locate the best part of the chosen region on which to build a city, appointing New South Wales Surveyor General Charles Scrivener to find out. Scrivener had been involved since 1901 in the search for a capital site. Now, based on the availability of water, wind exposure and amenability of the site to state-of-the-art sewering, he would determine exactly where the city would go. Scrivener headed a board that included the New South Wales government architect, Walter Liberty Vernon, the Commonwealth director general of works, Percy Owen, and the inaugural secretary of the Department of Home Affairs, David Miller.

Minister Mahon, who gets little credit for the choice of such a beautiful site, gave Scrivener a specific and visionary set of instructions. Mahon said Scrivener should consider

> that the Federal Capital should be a beautiful city, occupying a commanding position, with extensive views, and embracing distinctive features which will lend themselves to the evolution of a design worthy of the object, not only for the present, but for all time, consequently the potentialities of the site will demand most careful consideration from a scenic standpoint, with a view to securing picturesqueness, and also with the object of beautification and expansion.

Scrivener was a pragmatic, tough, results man. He was as handy with a shovel or at the camp oven as he was with a theodolite. He was utterly committed to public service and took a military approach to surveying and mapping out the colony of New South Wales, the state that followed and now the site of the federal capital.

His colleagues were men of precision, too. They were also genuine creatures of the military. Owen and Miller had both been Boer War commanders, while Vernon was a peacetime commander of the New South Wales Lancers and later the 1st Australian Light Horse Regiment. Colonels Miller and Owen both insisted on using their military honorifics in peacetime.

All felt great claim to the project – especially Miller, who regarded himself personally responsible for raising the capital as quickly as possible. Owen, Miller and Scrivener each developed strong views about where and how the city ought to be built through a framework more practical than aesthetic.

Scrivener established his 1909 survey camp beside Kurrajong Hill just below the Red Hill ridge line. A more permanent base camp was set up in the same place the next year; the camp stayed put for a further five years while surveyors mapped out the territory. Another camp for visiting members and senators was established nearby in 1910. In 1911, according to the Australian Bureau of Statistics, the Canberra district had about 1700 residents. Most lived on farms.

'The camp itself resembles an embryo mining camp with its rows of white fly tents and canvas bagging and corrugated iron structures for stables, kitchen and other temporary conveniences of camp life,' the Member for Lang, W.E. Johnson, wrote.

Johnson recalled that the plains below the camp were 'almost wholly given up to swarms of rabbits'.

During the MPs' visits, Colonel Miller ran the camps with military discipline. The MP Jimmy Catts said, 'if there is one special feature about the camp it is the strictly business appearance and military setting'.

In the six years of intensive surveying from 1909, Scrivener used a motorbike to get around. For the other members of the survey team the going was often very tough. Scrivener was a strict taskmaster. A hard exterior masking his geniality and sense of fun, Scrivener worked meticulously and methodically, sixteen hours, seven days a week. He demanded the same from subordinates.

One, Percy Sheaffe, wrote: 'In places the country encountered was so rough that the party carrying out the survey had to crawl on all fours, measure over precipices, and descend in one mile about 1550 feet.'

Scrivener completed his initial survey in just

two months, concluding the valley around the Molonglo, 'approaches nearer to what is required than any other I have inspected in the Yass–Canberra district'. While the survey team measured, Fisher's government fell. Deakin became prime minister for a third time. He governed for ten months, during which time the work of Scrivener and his board continued. Despite some wrangling with New South Wales over which water catchments would fall within the territory (briefly giving opponents a last hope that Yass–Canberra might be abandoned), a bill outlining the land that would have to be surrendered passed Parliament in December 1909.

Melbourne, which favoured the status quo whereby it was essentially the de facto capital, groaned. Sydney, however, saw an opportunity that finally transcended parochialism.

The Sydney Morning Herald of 27 November 1909 celebrated: 'Even though our capital be small, a unique opportunity offers for making it one of the most beautiful cities in the world.'

In April 1910 Fisher was re-elected prime minister. He appointed O'Malley minister for Home Affairs. Despite having been an ardent federalist and an early proponent of a bush capital, O'Malley had changed his tune as a backbencher, having settled comfortably in Melbourne – a city whose European culture and lifestyle he found congenial. But with characteristic unpredictability, upon assuming the ministry O'Malley immediately became the government's most passionate and vocal advocate of the capital that, he insisted, would be 'the finest city in the world'.

O'Malley took a caning in the Melbourne press, much of which excoriated the project. In October 1910 *The Argus* editorialised that the site for the new city was 'in a dip subject to intense heat, having a soil too poor for herbage and with no adequate source of water supply … no sane person would expend treasure and labour in trying to make a modern city in such surroundings'.

O'Malley countered: ' … we desire to have a city that will be the Gotham of Australia … [and] in a few years will rival London in size, Athens in art and Paris in beauty.'

Hyperbole aside, publicly O'Malley articulated a vision for a grand, permanent monument to the Australian federation and the ideals that it enshrined, including its progressive rights for workers, women's suffrage and high living standards. In reality, he knew nothing about town planning and had little idea of how to go about making a truly great city from scratch. He had no faith in the imagination of Colonel Miller who, he recognised, viewed the Department of Home Affairs as a personal fiefdom and ministers temporary obstacles best overcome with bureaucracy. Miller, who in 1912 would become the first administrator of the Federal Capital Territory, was a fierce and obstinate enemy. One of the surveyors, Arthur Percival, described him as 'gruff and frightening'.

Early in 1911 Fisher backed an idea (claimed as his own by O'Malley, even though it had been around for years) to hold an international competition for a capital design.

'If an Australian can produce a design, it will be accepted; but we require the best we can get, whether it comes from Swede or Dane, from Quaker, Shaker or Holy Roller,' O'Malley declared.

The competition courted instant international controversy. O'Malley appointed a Federal Capital Design Board to assess the designs and make recommendations. He refused to name the judges (but stipulated they would be Australian), and insisted on being the ultimate adjudicator. The Royal Institute of British Architects – which many Australian architects and planners viewed as their peak professional body – was angered by what it deemed to be an unprofessional judging process. While RIBA promptly boycotted the competition, entries nonetheless flooded in, including from British dominions.

Unperturbed, the obstinate O'Malley ordered his department to issue the guidelines. Competitors received a three-foot-long wooden box containing detailed material about the topography, climate, water catchments and features – including monumental buildings and the 'ornamental water' – that must be included. From the start of the search for a capital, water catchment – for the practical purposes of irrigation, potential electricity production, domestic supply and an aesthetically pleasing lake – was perhaps the most pressing prerequisite. Scrivener's earliest survey maps clearly provide for an artificial lake; ornamental water had been central to the design vision long before the competition was launched.

Each box also contained detailed contour maps, a geological map of the region, and two cyclorama reproductions by Charles Coulter (of that grand 1901 vision of the Lake George capital) depicting the site from Capital Hill and what would become another corner of the land axis at City Hill. (Coulter also entered the design competition.)

Plaster models of the site were displayed in major cities, including London, Washington, Ottowa, Paris, Berlin and Chicago. The deadline was 31 January 1912, later extended to 28 February 1912.

In Chicago, Walter Griffin and his new wife Marion Mahony Griffin (they married while preparing their design) collected their box and viewed the plaster model. The prodigious Griffin – once a disciple of the great Chicago architect Frank Lloyd Wright and his 'Prairie School' of simple, elegant domestic building – had long been anticipating the competition for the capital. Griffin was captivated by Australia's quick and peaceful evolution into a federation, and he had been waiting for the opportunity to design a capital that would encapsulate the optimism and ideals of the new Australia – a city, he said, for a country of 'bold democrats'.

The influences on Griffin were eclectic. Chief among them was the City Beautiful Movement of the late nineteenth century. The movement was underpinned by a desire to match the notion of architecturally sculpted monumental buildings in natural landscapes with dignified medium-density suburbs (a departure from the squalid, unplanned high-density slums that characterised the big cities) where street life would coexist with some retail and entertainment facilities. The World Columbian Exhibition of 1893 in Chicago had a significant formative influence on Griffin, even if the 'City' part of City Beautiful did receive disproportionate emphasis; some were shocked by the stark contrast between the sprawling, splendid exhibition site and the squalor of the slums nearby.

In his design for Canberra, Griffin drew heavily on City Beautiful. But he was also influenced by elements of the parallel Garden City Movement that interlaced built-up urban areas with corridors of countryside and communal recreation areas. The Griffins were driven by a philosophy that domestic architecture could not be approached in isolation; the natural environment, human welfare and, perhaps most importantly, community interactions, had to be the guiding principles.

Griffin weighted his plan with land and water axes, dividing the city into government, municipal, education, market and military sectors. While the distant ranges would be the backdrop for the city, the internal hills and slopes would be the podiums for symbolic, monumental buildings of importance, such as his Capitol, the Parliament, the City Hall and his greatly misunderstood Casino, which stands in the drawings on the rise below Mount Ainslie. The design imposed an alluring geometric order on the landscape, along wide avenues that he envisaged would brim with residential and commercial life, around the monumental buildings that symbolised the fledgling Australian federation.

Griffin struggled to articulate his vision for the capital, and had procrastinated in his Chicago office for weeks until Marion had pushed him to start. She, after all, was the artist who would draw his vision in fifteen pictures, fourteen of them exquisite watercolour-rendered prints that would be regarded internationally, though tellingly not in Australia, as precious artworks.

'For the love of Mike!' Marion, five years her husband's senior, admonished him as the deadline neared. 'When are you going to get started on those capital plans? Perhaps you can design a city in two days but the drawing takes time and that falls on me.'

Griffin was a visionary. But he was a lousy draughtsman. Marion was perhaps the best architectural drawer in the world at the time. Heavily influenced by contemporary Japanese decorative and landscape art, her beautifully composed drawings were renowned for perfectly capturing architectural objects in their natural contexts.

The Griffins completed their entry in just nine weeks and had a last-minute rush to get it onto the boat for Australia. Marion's most famous image is a triptych depicting their imagined view of the city from Mount Ainslie. It was finished too late for the boat. Instead, Marion sent a more functional drawing depicting the same perspective and identifying, probably in Marion's writing, the city's major buildings.

Marion penned an apology in black ink on a lower corner of the drawing: 'PERSPECTIVE DRAWING HAS BEEN DELAYED BY ACCIDENT. WILL BE SENT BY NEXT SHIPMENT.'

The coloured triptych arrived a few weeks later, after which the black-and-white annotated copy disappeared.

It would not turn up until almost a century later, in 2011. Its significance is still being realised by the legions of architecture and town planning academics and Griffin experts who've pored over the couple's work.

The judging board was divided, but it named Griffin the majority winner on 23 May 1912. O'Malley backed the decision.

A perfunctory telegram informed Griffin: 'Your

design awarded first premium. Minister Home Affairs.'

Later that day, Griffin responded: 'Thanks for notification. Honor appreciated.'

An understated response, yes. Griffin had taken a keen interest in Australian federation and, since the late nineteenth century, its debate over the siting and possible contruction of a capital. He was always going to enter any design contest. Supremely confident in his talents, this was the result he had probably anticipated.

Third place was awarded to the French architect Donat Alfred Agache, who pitched a formal European-style city through which a wild, ungainly Molonglo meandered, much as the Seine does within Paris. Second was Finnish architect Eliel Saarinen. Saarinen produced an elaborately rendered – almost futuristic – city on the water, of many integrating and heavily engineered watercourses, canals, pools and lakes that he lined with tightly grouped buildings that were more appropriate to an extreme cold climate. It was beautiful but showed little affinity with the site.

I had seen copies of the Mahony–Griffin design pictures displayed at various times in Canberra. But never the curious 'missing' line drawing that was rediscovered in 2011. And I wanted to know what it meant.

I drive out to Mitchell, a semi-industrial northern suburb of Canberra where the National Archives of Australia stores most of its collection. The warehouse is a vast above-ground concrete bunker of elephant-hide hue and rough texture. It is functional, as befits Mitchell – a dusty utilitarian estate standing amid yellowing pastures somewhere out near the cemetery and crematorium, hemmed in by roads connecting Canberra's satellites.

Ian Batterham, a senior curator for the Archives, meets me.

He tells me how a few years ago he wrote an article about his restoration of the Griffins' Canberra pictures and what happened to the images after they won the design contest. The original pictures were drawn on silk tracing cloth, probably with a nibbed pen, he explains.

It was a painstaking and meticulous process; the pressure on the silk had to be gossamer-light so the nib didn't tear the delicate fabric or blot. From the original monochrome ink drawing on linen, Marion made lithographs on window shade Holland fabric that she rendered and annotated with watercolour, photographic dye and red ink. A third stage of the drawings – lithographs on satin – the Griffins kept for themselves.

The Holland lithographs were stretched onto frames for the competition. Thirteen coloured drawings made it in time for the deadline. The fourteenth – the famous triptych – was slightly later, the black-and-white line drawing (known as 'drawing fifteen') having been sent temporarily in its place to meet O'Malley's deadline.

After the competition, the Griffins' stage three prints – the satin lithographs – were sent to Europe and, appropriately, displayed as art. Their whereabouts remains unknown.

In his 2009 article in the German publication *Restaurator* Batterham mentioned that the 'make-do image' Marion initially sent instead of the triptych 'was either destroyed or lost'.

Soon after the article was published, he took a phone call from Dr David Headon, a Canberra-based historian who is dedicated to unearthing stories about Canberra's evolution. Headon is a gifted orator and laconic writer. He is Australia's foremost expert on the symbolism and political genesis of the national capital. He is the historical adviser for the 2013 centenary commemoration.

For a few days after visiting the Planning Institute of Australia, Headon carried around a swathe of old documents regarding Canberra's planning. Batterham's article prompted him to inspect more closely the documents and other material, still in his car, that he'd borrowed from the institute. There was a non-descript cardboard cylinder. When he unrolled Marion's black-and-white line drawing of the view from Mount Ainslie, he immediately knew what it was (he and Batterham had both seen a photograph of the document that was taken when the competition entries arrived in 1912).

Headon rang Batterham: 'I've found the missing picture.'

'I've described it as an absolute Eureka moment. I was really moved to have accidentally rediscovered the image … the planning institute did not know what it was that had just been sitting there.'

Headon explains its significance:

> The really interesting thing about it is that they went through the whole drawing and annotated it with the names of each building. The real

> uniqueness of this is that it is the only place that they did that. So it shows you where they wanted the High Court, for example, the Parliament roughly where the Old Provisional Parliament is and the Capitol up on the hill – and of course the casino.

Batterham takes me deep into the Archives building in Mitchell. The 'missing' drawing should have been preserved for decades as it is now – in carefully humidified and temperature-controlled storage.

'The paper is very acidic and because it's been so badly stored, it is now extremely brittle.'

He shows me a true-to-scale photograph of the drawing, complete with Marion's 'late note' in the corner.

I'm moved: this, more than any of Marion's other images of the capital – as beautiful as they are – was, as she created it, more than just a brilliant annotated vision of their perfect capital. It was a roadmap that foresaw the high-collision areas for her husband and the Australian authorities. It is the map of what was already a lost dream.

In the third of the 'Edith Trilogy' novels, *Cold Light,* Frank Moorhouse's heroine Edith Campbell Berry, disillusioned after the collapse of the League of Nations, comes to Canberra in the 1950s. She takes an ill-defined public service position as an assistant to Trevor Gibson, the first appointed town planner of Canberra. Gibson is trying, under direction from Prime Minister Robert Menzies, to kick-start what was then a failing capital experiment.

Moorhouse conjures a passage in Gibson's office in the National Capital Development Commission at Acton. Berry sees for the first time Marion's drawings – grey-greens, ochres, golds, browns and russets.

'I got them over from the Department of Works. They're a bit dusty. I wanted to have a quick look at them. Not much use,' Gibson tells her.

Gibson explains there are more pictures of the surpassed Griffin design 'over in one of the Nissen huts'. Like so much of the Moorhouse trilogy, the fictitious Berry has been written into an historically accurate landscape, for Gibson is referring to a storage shed in which the Griffin plans had actually been effectively discarded from the 1920s until the early 1950s.

In 1913 the Griffin illustrations were removed from their frames, rolled up and stored in cylinders. Griffin recommended that the pictures be conserved in the same way as paintings; they were reframed and kept in custom-made zinc-lined chests. Nobody heard of them until 1953 when they turned up in five wooden crates in a work shed in Kingston. In 1957 they were moved to the Nissen storage huts in Parkes.

In *Cold Light,* Berry 'looked at them one by one, mounted on chipboard backings … "They're rather magnificent."'

Berry thought the illustrations asked 'to be respectfully touched in the same way that they had been so assiduously created'.

Representing, perhaps, the most generous view of most of the planners from 1911 until at least the 1950s who had come in contact with them, Gibson says he thinks they 'are rather good in a dreamy way'. He continued:

> 'Griffin's plans – surpassed now. Remember, they were done before air travel, before everyone could own the motorcar, before the *autobahn* or the super highway. Although you'd think from the plans that we all flew like birds and that was how we would always look at the city – from a bird's eye view or from an aeroplane.' And he added with a kind of distrust, 'And all that statutory pattern.'

Berry responds that the plans 'say more than they depict'.

> She then turned to the plans. 'And we will see the city from above – from Red Hill, from Mount Ainslie. From "lookouts". And we will pretty soon all be flying in and out of Canberra. Thankfully, no American skyscrapers.' She said the plans were a sort of geometric artistry. 'Griffin would say "severe simplicity". The city should be like a fine sculpture – it should be pleasing when looked at from any angle.'

Berry, like Moorhouse, understood Griffin's Canberra, forecasting how so many of us today might, when we look down from our chosen heights about the place, vividly imagine Marion's triptych superimposed over the skeletal remains of Walter's geometry.

In 1957 the pictures were sent to the Art Gallery of New South Wales for treatment. They were sent to a commercial framer who cut off the white borders of the triptych and glued the three parts directly onto masonite. In 1965 the pictures were stripped from the masonite and glued onto chipboard. In the late 1980s Batterham began the years-long process of removing the pictures from the chipboard, repairing, cleaning, mounting and framing them once more. It was, he says, particularly difficult to remove the instructions that had been written in crayon or heavy lead pencil directly onto the backs of the works when they had been 'treated' twice by commercial framers.

Batterham wrote in *Restaurator*:

> All of the drawings were generally very dirty and most had scuff marks, finger marks and losses of gold and other paint. Comparison to early photographs showed that many of the drawings had faded considerably, of particular note was the right hand portion of the triptych which had lost much of its colour, as if wiped away by a damp cloth – it is not known when or how this happened.

It is not hard to see the blasé treatment of Marion's illustrations as a metaphor for how the Australian officials responsible for the building of Canberra came to view and treat the Griffins.

Two months after winning the competition, Griffin told *The New York Times* he had 'planned a city not like any other city the world ... an ideal city – a city that meets my ideal of the city of the future'.

But it was never Griffin's city. Even before the competition was announced some small buildings were going up on the as yet unnamed capital site. The competition guidelines were ambiguous about whether the city should occupy both sides of the Molonglo. Griffin's vision straddled the sculptured ornamental lake that would form from the dammed Molonglo, with his government group (including Parliament and the Capitol) and the military to the south, and the recreational group (including the zoo, a casino and an opera house) to the north near Mount Ainslie. His plan put a central railway station in the civic sector, north of the lake. He also specified a series of residential communities, each in a triangular precinct of between twelve and twenty-five acres. Most residents were to be housed in terraces, each with a front and rear garden for privacy and ventilation. The suburban centres would be carefully linked to each other and to the central areas of the city by a series of radiating avenues. Residents would have space, but they would not be isolated in suburbia under this plan. Bigger bungalow-style houses surrounded by gardens would be reserved for the steeper hillside allotments at the edges of town.

It would all be linked by an elaborate tramway system along the wide boulevard-style avenues that would, it was anticipated, attract business. The internal geometry of Griffin's design would hang on a land axis that divided the triangle formed by Kings Avenue and Commonwealth Avenue, with their bridges across the lake, and later Constitution Avenue at right angles just beyond the lake's northern shore.

Griffin sited his recreational buildings on the north, on either side of the land axis, so that they might form a symbolic audience for the triangular government group with its apex at the Capitol. Marion drew a 600-foot-wide park – the Midway Pleasance – along the remainder of the land axis at the northern flank of the lake (and the edge of the civic centre) to the foot of Mount Ainslie. There, the casino (never properly described by Griffin who dropped the concept in 1915, but understood by experts on his work to be an open-air 'pleasure garden' incorporating a theatre, small restaurants, stalls and a beer garden) would stand, emphasising the end of the land axis that connected the man-made government sector and lake with a natural full point – Mount Ainslie.

Australian planners, politicians and bureaucrats – especially the crusty colonels overseeing the capital project – were not much interested in 'Continental'-style medium-density living, combined with shopping and al fresco dining such as the Griffin plan encouraged. They wanted their bungalows girt by garden – not terraces – to live in. They certainly didn't want casinos – whatever they were!

Dr Karl Fischer, a German Professor of Planning who teaches at the University of Kassel, told me the German-style beer garden was probably fundamental to Griffin's image of the northern end of his 'pleasance' – his 'playground of the city' – abutting Mount Ainslie.

'In the early 1890s there were thirty German newspapers in Chicago and a number of German theaters, not to mention the Beer Gardens. The beer gardens were a model for Lloyd Wright's 1913 Midway Gardens entertainment precinct on Chicago's lakefront, and also more than likely for the Casino which Griffin proposed for the northern end of his Midway Pleasance,' says Fischer, who has been studying the urban design of Canberra for more than twenty years.

It is fair to assume that O'Malley – who railed against alcohol during his public life – would have disapproved.

From early 1911, O'Malley had given assurances the capital would be alcohol-free. The Independent Order of Rechabites had protested to Prime Minister Fisher and O'Malley about the likely location of a hotel in the capital. O'Malley assured it would be a temperance institution. Today there's no shortage of places to drink in Canberra; licensed clubs and restaurants, small bars and nightclubs are scattered throughout the suburban shopping strips and town centres. But thanks to O'Malley, there are very few pubs – let alone old ones – in Canberra.

Meanwhile, the main symbolic feature of Griffin's design, the proposed Capitol building on the peak of Kurrajong (later Capital) Hill, was as inarticulately explained as it was badly understood.

The Capitol was intended to be the most symbolically democratic of the buildings on the plan – a place, as Griffin put it, for popular reception and ceremony, 'or for housing archives and commemorating Australian achievements rather than for deliberation or counsel; at any rate representing the sentimental and spiritual head, if not the actual working mechanism of the federation'. It was a place where the Australian story could be told.

The Capitol's stepped ziggurat stands eighty feet above the summit of the hill, flanked by residences for both the prime minister and the governor-general. The people would be above the executive and the head of state.

'Neither the Griffins nor anyone else ever managed to set down a clear description of this institution that was to be the climax of the capital and thus of the nation,' wrote Paul Reid in *Canberra Following Griffin*. 'It became an early target of Griffin critics.'

Of whom there were many.

O'Malley effusively praised the winning design, saying Australia had 'wanted ... the best the world could give us and we got it'.

But he was soon pandering to the political and media cynicism: the design was too elaborate, esoteric and, not least, too costly.

Both Griffin and Mahony dabbled in eastern philosophy and mysticism. Mahony was an adherent of theosophy and a devotee of Rudolph Steiner's anthroposophy. Griffin, with his long hair and penchant for soft collars and loose, exuberant neckwear, and Marion, who exuded a Pre-Raphaelite composure and mystique, looked, sounded and most significantly, thought, differently to the Australian political elite who were still tied to Empire. The Griffins were also vocal pacifists and Germanophiles as the world was inching closer towards war with the German Realm.

O'Malley reminded Australia that his competition reserved the right to cherry-pick from winning plans to find a final satisfactory design. And so in June 1912 he referred the three winning plans and another design – by the Australians Robert Coulter (of the 1901 Lake George vision), W. Scott Griffiths and Charles Caswell – to a departmental board.

The board comprised, among others, Scrivener, Owen and John Murdoch – the Department of Home Affairs senior architect who would go on to design and build many of early Canberra's most famous, striking and interesting buildings.

Colonel Miller headed the board.

In late November 1912 the board announced it could not wholly recommend any of the plans.

It came up with its own bastardised hybrid that stole Griffin's land axis, kept his Capitol as a beacon on Kurrajong but concentrated the city south of the Molonglo, meshing the municipal, the residential and the government. O'Malley immediately accepted it.

Griffin, appalled, offered to come out to Australia to straighten out 'unresolved plan problems'. Owen and Murdoch thought it a good idea. But Miller, who was now living in Canberra and eager to start building, let it be known Griffin was neither required nor wanted.

On 20 February 1913 O'Malley drove the first peg into the dusty rabbit-infested site with an upturned axe, while the public wondered what name would be given to the capital when the foundation stone was laid the next month. The possibilities seemed endless: Sydmelperadbrisho, Wheatwoolgold, Kangaremu, Eucalypta, Thirstyville, Shakespeare, Myola (favoured, it was said, by the prime minister), Malleyking, Fisherburra and Circle City were all suggested.

On 12 March the *Sydney Mail* published a photograph of a vast barren moonscape devoid of human interference and featuring two dead trees and a lone dog. It was captioned 'The site that Australia Selected for its Capital: A General View Taken a Few Days Ago'.

Five thousand people came to the Limestone Plains on 12 March 1913. The mist quickly burnt off, making way for a wave of dust that enveloped the site, courtesy of the arrival by car and horse-drawn carriage of out-of-towners and locals.

The locals knew that they stood to have their land compulsorily acquired for the new capital. Some, like the Campbells of Duntroon, had already sold part of their landholdings for good prices. Since 1911, Duntroon had been the Royal Military Academy – the place where future warriors would learn how to lead men and make war. But smaller farmers, many of whom were descendants of the pioneering settlers, would struggle to win a fair price.

A grandstand was erected high on Kurrajong for the 500 officially invited guests. They would look north across the plains towards Mount Ainslie, and down upon the foundation stone that was intended to be the base of an unsightly phallus-like column. The great base, comprising six stones – each representing an Australian state – was planted in the middle of a 'Peoples' Park' that, in Griffin's drawing, surrounded what would be the most important building in the land – his Capitol. It was intended that an eight-metre, four-sided obelisk (representing the four corners of the British Empire) would stand on the foundation stone. But

World War I austerity would put an end to that – and much else about the Canberra plan.

About a thousand members of the 3rd Australian Light Horse Brigade stood at attention, forming a square in front of the grandstand. The dust and pollen played havoc with the hay fever and asthma of Governor-General Lord Thomas Denman who, in a speech (purportedly written by Miller himself) gave credit to Miller, Owen and Scrivener, while ignoring Griffin. He expressed hope that future Australian governments would find 'inspiration' in the city's 'noble buildings, its broad avenues, its shaded parks and sheltered gardens'. To which plan, I wonder was he – or more correctly Miller – referring? Griffin's or the department's?

Miller wore full military uniform. Fisher, Lord Denman and O'Malley then used individual gold trowels to tap the stones of the commencement column into place. At exactly midday O'Malley's wife Amy handed Lady Denman a small gold case. It contained a card on which was written the hitherto secret name of the new capital.

Lady Denman made the long-awaited announcement: 'I name the capital of Australia, Canberra.' Then she added: 'The accent is on the can.'

It was CANberra – Ngambri – then.

The Peoples' Park never eventuated. Griffin's Capitol was never built. There is still no foundation column.

But Canberra's first monument was laid. It would be moved slightly down the northern face of Capital Hill in 1988 to make way for the new Parliament House, where it would stand in a pivotal place – geographically and symbolically – as Australia passed its bicentenary.

In May 1913 Fisher's Labor government lost office. Fisher's successor, Joseph Cook, delegated the Home Affairs portfolio to William Kelly. Kelly immediately contacted Griffin, who came to Australia to meet the board. Griffin revised his initial plan, saving on costs by concentrating his city south of the Molonglo (although surreptitiously ensuring it could expand to the north by insisting on two of five bridges he had originally planned, across the Molonglo). Kelly dismissed the board and appointed Griffin as Federal Capital Director of Design and Construction.

Griffin went home to sort out his business

commitments, arriving back in May 1914 just months before the outbreak of World War I. Miller and others did their best in his absence to undermine Griffin with the new government, and continued to build their small capital south of the river beginning with the power station in the heart of what Griffin had envisaged would be a residential area. (It is fitting that the heated politics of Canberra planning has its physical manifestation at this spot. Today, bitter local argument surrounds the future use of the fitter's workshop next to the power station in the Kingston visual arts precinct. The concrete, gable-roofed building has long been earmarked for a printmaking studio, but others insist it is of rare acoustic quality and should be reserved for some forms of musical performance.)

Griffin held the job until Prime Minister Billy Hughes effectively sacked him in late 1920. During this time there was a royal commission into Canberra that found Griffin had achieved virtually nothing – but had also been constantly undermined.

During the war years, a ludicrous situation had evolved. Griffin was still redesigning his heavily amended plan for the capital while the public servants were ignoring him and actually building theirs south of the river. They were determined to abandon the lake on the basis of cost.

In 1915 the architect George Taylor, under the headline 'The Fight for Canberra', wrote in *Building* magazine:

> The story of Canberra is the story of a bungle ... The shadow of the 'government stroke' is over everything. Workmen seem to do things when they like, and pretty nearly how they like, with no regard to recognized authority, or any ordered system. Some have been seen endeavouring to work under the influence of liquor ... A great power station was also dumped, at a cost of 60,000 pounds, on a site near what is intended to be the residential quarter of the city. The minister stated, however: – 'It will be no serious matter if two or three temporary buildings on a street or an intended street disappear during the next five years; much more important matters concern us'.

Griffin's 1918 plan, as emasculated as it had become, was gazetted in 1925 at the behest of Stanley Melbourne Bruce, whose contribution to the development of Canberra is rarely mentioned. But Bruce – Australia's youngest PM and the first of two incumbents (the other was John Howard) to lose his seat at an election – was just as energetic a champion of the capital as Menzies would be in the 1950s. He oversaw in the 1920s what remains, proportionately, the most significant phase of Canberra's early development, and imposed his will on the bureaucrats of the Federal Capital Advisory Committee and its successor, the Federal Capital Commission, who had made life so difficult for Griffin. Bruce was heavily influenced by his attorney general, Littleton Groom, who, as Works minister under Hughes, had fought for Griffin's plan. Groom considered following the bones of the Griffin plan the best way ahead. Ironically, Groom terminated Griffin in 1920; he believed in his plan but thought – probably correctly – the American too impractical and intransigent to actually build the city. Groom, incidentally, is buried at St John's.

Bruce and Groom were determined the Australian capital would, in accordance with the Constitution, be built. They wanted a permanent plan for the city so they could not be hoodwinked – as successive previous administrations had been – by the planning and building bureaucrats who were driven by their entrenched views about the city and their animosity towards Griffin and his plans. Gazettal meant the plan could no longer be altered without parliamentary approval. This was essentially a formality; the planning bureaucrats could simply submit proposed changes to the minister who would then, if convinced, usher them through Parliament. Given that most MPs had no idea what was in the Griffin plan, the bureaucrats had the permanent upper hand. The gazetted 'plan' was little more than a broad blueprint – a series of lines, representing roads, that made no reference to Griffin's zoning and detailed layout preferences. But it was all that remained.

With its two bridges and sculpted lake included, it would form the basis of future planning for the city. But it was a shadow of the beautifully rendered 1911 plan that Griffin described as 'an expression of the democratic civic ideal and all that means in accessibility, freedom, wealth, comfort, convenience, scale and splendour'.

Griffin walked away from Canberra in 1920. He spoke of it occasionally as a lost opportunity, but largely without rancour.

In notes for a 1928 speech he wrote:

> In 1911 I made a plan for Canberra, which finally after a seven years battle with the authorities was adopted by the Federal Parliament in 1921 (though not gazetted until 1925). However, the town planning determinents embodies [sic] in that paper plan were not recognized and the administering authorities from the beginning have violated the aesthetic, social and economic principles in almost every set and the structural details for roads, bridges, locks, weirs, railways, sewerage, water supply, electric power and gas services which was worked out as part and parcel of that plan ... have never even been referred to in the actual work.

In other words, the authorities simply began building to their ideas, leaving Griffin to finesse his plan – which they largely ignored.

As if such bureaucratic stonewalling were not enough, between his appointment and departure in 1920, Griffin was forced to work with another five governments (including three led by Billy Hughes) and five more Home Affairs ministers, including, once again, O'Malley.

Marion was angry on her husband's behalf.

In *The Magic of America*, Mahony's tribute to life with her husband, she reproduced a letter to her friend, Australian novelist Stella 'Miles' Franklin.

'As to the plan they have no notion of letting any plan but their own be carried into execution and as they are in power for life they can gain their ends, they hope, by delay piled on delay ...'

She described Griffin's time as director as 'a perpetual battle one might say, against an Empire' and 'continual warfare'.

Later she wrote to friends: 'The one word that describes the methods here is inefficiency and the one that describes the ideal is mediocrity.'

She railed against the public servants, one of whom had said to Walter, 'I'll be damned if I'll take orders from you,' upon his appointment, and she wrote of the 'marked difference in the ideals of Australians and Americans; the Australian's ideal aristocracy, the American's democracy; the Australian interest in getting out of doing, the American's in doing'.

David Headon points out that Griffin's opponents had made an enormous personal investment in the capital project since before federation. While they clearly resented the imposition of an outsider, he believes they were better equipped than Griffin to determine what could realistically be built.

> You've got to see the human dimension of this. Here this guy turns up. He's … a pacifist and it's World War I. And Owen, Miller and Vernon are former Boer War colonels. And this guy's a mid-western hippy. There's just no way they're going to get along. So you've got this extraordinary clash of wills and background and philosophy and in some ways that's constantly coming to a head.

Dorothy Adams was a little girl in the crowd when Lady Denman named Canberra.

'There are pictures of the historic day … and if you look closely on the right handside, on the stand erected for sightseeing, you will see two girls, me and Letty Kay. It was apparently a public holiday.'

She and her parents arrived on the Limestone Plains about 1909 after her father, a miner, failed to find gold at Cowra Creek in the Great Dividing Range.

In an unpublished memoir of her Canberra childhood she wrote: 'Our "promised land" Canberra was, a place of rolling plains, green grass and a west wind always blowing. Hot and dry in the summer and bitterly cold in the winter, with the everlasting wind blowing over the frost-covered ground.'

In later years, amid her recollections of Samuel Shumack's stories about Canberra ghosts and a bone-dry Lake George, she alluded to the social divisions between wealthy landowners and tenant farmers.

'It was the home of the Campbells of Duntroon and most of the people living there thought of it that way, most of them being tenants.' When Canberra was built and the land compulsorily acquired, great wealth was bestowed upon 'people who wanted and had been given land, the people like the Campbells, to whom the government felt it owed a debt of gratitude.

'Then there were others who were brave enough to leave civilisation and face the hardships of hard work and of the unknown.'

She recalled the first public servants moving reluctantly from Melbourne a few years after the surveyors began their work.

> The Lands Office was the first to be built
> followed by various departments as they
> were needed, a post office, a branch of the

> Commonwealth bank, bachelors quarters for the single men of the public service – they were not very happy, there was nothing interesting for them to do in their time, not theatres … no pubs, Queanbeyan on Saturday afternoon and evening provided this but they had to get there and this was a time when not everyone had cars.
>
> Surveyors were every[where] and scars marred the landscape as foundation buildings appeared. Most of the big landowners had had their land acquired and departed. No longer did the Campbells of Yarralumla arrive at the Church in their carriage and pair …

Griffin was not the only one ignored. Adams said the engineers didn't heed the advice of locals when building the first bridge across the river.

> Came the first flood and the bridge was gone. They built a slightly larger one, the same thing happened then they realised that what they had been told by old residents was true. This time they built a bridge that was strong and with the approach stretching across the flats that the flood waters always covered. They would still be underwater but the bridge withstood the challenge.

> The nursery was planted and soon filled with the trees and flowering shrubs that would later adorn the streets of the city. A powerhouse was built … and soon lights began to appear among the trees.

But World War I had effectively flicked the light switch off.

Barely three months after Griffin returned to Australia to oversee Canberra's construction, Australia joined Britain in the war against Germany and its allies.

Most of the public servants were sent back to the states, where many eagerly joined the battalions and the regiments that were being hastily raised in the belief that it would all be over in months.

The war would last four years and three months. It would kill, maim and otherwise scar an entire Australian generation. Very few of those who returned would ever be the same, physically, emotionally or psychologically.

It would maim the infant Canberra, too.

Continuing City

Like much about early Canberra, politics also heavily compromised the most important building in the intended seat of federal democracy – Parliament House.

Griffin had supported an international design competition for Parliament House to be built, on Camp Hill on the land axis immediately below Capital Hill. The government called for competitors on 1 July 1914. Five weeks later, the war began, making it impossible to mount a truly 'international competition' (potential designers from 'enemy' countries would have to be banned, automatically giving competitive advantage to others).

Ultimately, the competition for a permanent Parliament House was postponed until 1980.

During the war, Griffin continued his battle of attrition with the bureaucrats, trying to save the essence of his 1912 city plan while the officials built their small city south of the Molonglo.

Australia emerged from the war in November 1918 with a debt of £364 million and an urgent requirement to repatriate about 350 000 returned soldiers. By the early 1920s, Parliament House, like Canberra generally, had become a question of simple aspiration: should Australia make it a permanent building or delay the associated costs and decisions by going for a temporary option? In 1923 Parliament chose, probably judiciously given the state of the economy, to go for a temporary one that would suffice for two or three decades. It would do so for sixty-one years.

The minister for Works and Railways, Percy Stewart, explained, perhaps defensively:

> … it will in no way be a mean structure. While its design is on simple and economic lines, it will be substantially constructed in brick and will be of commodious and comfortable character, presenting a good appearance architecturally … The design includes garden courts, and conforms to the general conception of Canberra in the first stage as a garden city.

At once ornate and unpretentious, the 'wedding cake' as it's still known, was something of a design triumph. It was also a testimony to the superhuman deadline capacity of Commonwealth architect John Murdoch. Murdoch was by all accounts belting out the design drawings for the external structure and interior fittings as quickly as the director of Works, Colonel Percy Owen, could knock up the building itself.

'We are getting nervous that we will overtake the drawings unless you can let us have something more to go on with next week,' Owen wrote to Murdoch in February 1924.

Canberra had been dormant during the war. Despite the parsimony underscoring post-war public spending, Canberra's development enjoyed a short sharp burst of activity for about seven years from 1922. Contract labourers and skilled tradesmen – hundreds upon hundreds of war veterans among them – descended on Canberra. Besides Parliament House, they built Hostel Number One as the main residence for the politicians, and the adjacent Albert Hall that would quickly become the civic heart of the early city (Griffin's planned city hall on the north side did not, like his imposing central train station, happen). The bungalow-style hostel and Albert Hall were sited on Commonwealth Avenue precisely where

Griffin had planned medium-density terrace housing and shops. The hall symbolised optimism that a community could and would grow around – and indeed out of – the construction of a governmental seat.

It was a proud show of faith in a continuing city.

A brickworks, linked by rail to the powerhouse and Parliament House site, was punching out 'Canberra reds' just as fast as they could be laid into the framework of the hall, the hostel, the nearby Kurrajong Hotel, the Commonwealth's earliest on-site administration buildings and its all-important sewerage system.

Camps of varying descriptions and degrees of comfort sprung up about the plains and foothills as men, more often than not *sans* families, came to pick up the work.

The camps sprung up around Eastlake and the 'causeway' that was never built – but was still called Causeway – on the east of the Molonglo floodplain. They also dotted the ridge below Acton and the valley opposite at Westlake.

Some camps were strategically located so that they could not easily be seen – or offend – those at Parliament House and at Hostel Number One (known after 1927 as Hotel Canberra; now the Hyatt). Commonwealth Avenue effectively tapered off into two gravel tracks towards Kurrajong, on either side of the hotel.

The 1925 Christmas edition of the magazine *Canberra Illustrated* effusively promoted the capital's abundant natural beauty and rapid growth. While the magazine did not go out of its way to highlight the city's underbelly of boozing and violence, it did question the rapid emergence of – and widening gulf between – the city's social classes.

A D.B. O'Connor lyrically described the Hostel Number One's 'commodious' charms:

> With its spacious ball room, lounge, smoke and card rooms, its lovely dining room, bedroom suites, billiard parlours and up to date culinary department, this hotel is probably the finest place of its kind in the South Pacific. In the grounds along side are tennis and croquet lawns and the first hole of the golf links is within five minutes' walk.

It was centrally heated, each room had running hot and cold water, a garage to service motor cars, and undercover parking for thirty-eight vehicles.

The magazine reported that Thomas Weston, the federal capital's horticulturalist who oversaw the planting of close to two million trees during his fourteen years in the job, took special interest in the gardens of the hotel. He planted 25 000 tulips in the grounds and another 20 000 rose bushes in the gardens between the hotel, Commonwealth Avenue and the Albert Hall.

The floral blooms must have presented a rare splash of beauty for the men of the camps, 700 of whom – or about a fifth of the capital's total population – now lived at Westlake, in the gulley along the Molonglo and down from the hostel.

The Christmas 1925 edition of *Canberra Illustrated* was its first and last. It never entirely understood its readers, although it was certainly curious about the emerging contradictions in the city, supposedly a monument to the great egalitarian dream.

Like everywhere else, Hotel Canberra was 'dry' thanks to O'Malley, whose ill-conceived prohibition remained in force until 1928. Dry in all but practice, that is. How appropriate that today we can toast the American's memory with a stagger juice or two at 'King O'Malley's', a Canberra bar that rocks and sways in his memory.

Illegal alcohol was the recreational bedrock for

the thousands of workmen who passed through the camps each year. Politics, too, always lubricated with strong drink, demanded more than the capital could offer. The many politicians who visited brought their own supplies or frequented Queanbeyan, where a pub graced practically every corner and each block between. It's said some politicians, drawn to the prospect of edgy entertainment, might have sometimes visited the camps where drink, gambling and licentiousness were rife.

Early residents of suburbs such as Blandfordia (later Forrest) would recall a stream of car lights heading east towards Queanbeyan at dusk.

Gay and George Sykes ran the first taxi service from Westlake. Most passengers went to Queanbeyan to drink solidly, and returned with bottles.

Horrie Cleaver ran Westlake's first hire car service. Business was flat out from about 4 pm Friday when workers would take to Queanbeyan's pubs for the weekend.

An old Westlake resident, Charlie Law, later recalled: 'The onerous task of searching all the hotels in Queanbeyan for the men to come home would often take all day on the Sunday.'

Accommodation was scarce for labourers and tradesmen. An internment camp (known as a 'concentration camp' in the district) for Germans had been established in May 1918 at an isolated spot on the south-eastern bank of the Molonglo. The internment camp and its hospital operated for less than a year before being transformed into accommodation for 120 married and 150 single labourers.

Today, it is Fyshwick. On Griffin's plan, Fyshwick was Canberra's intended Mosman or Kew, perched above the rest of the city so it might look down along the axis of water when the lake came into being. But the colonels knocking Canberra together built their powerhouse in Kingston. It needed fuel, so the railway line was extended from Queanbeyan and the fuel storage depots inevitably ended up along the railway line at Fyshwick.

So, 'Fyshwick' and 'desirable residential property' have never been exactly synonymous. One of two places in Canberra (the other is Mitchell) where prostitution can operate legally, Fyshwick caters to many different desires. In the late 80s and 90s it hosted another burgeoning arm of the sex industry – X-rated pornography, which can be legally sold in Canberra. Fyshwick became home to Australia's first porn supermarkets, which were marketed, prosaically, as places where liberated couples and their friends could shop for erotic lingerie, inflatable friends, magazines, potions and lotions and the mainstay of XXX – videos, and later, DVDs. (In truth, they were magnets for furtive-looking single older men and blokes on footy trips.) Canberra's bordellos still do a roaring trade, so it is said, during parliamentary sittings and events such as the annual Summernats car festival. But as a producer, wholesaler and mail order retailer of XXX, it is dying, a victim of the internet.

But semi-industrial Fyshwick has long been more than just the home of porn. In the course of an average year I am likely to return from Fyshwick with: pool chemicals; computer hardware; a dishwasher part; sporting shoes; a new pillow; a child's birthday present; bulk dog food; oysters; wine; jeans; spectacles; a throw for the sofa; seedlings; stationery; firewood; hinges and nails; paint and sandpaper.

Fyshwick is home to the best array of second-hand bookshops in the city, and sells the most exceptional sourdough and chicken pies in the ACT. You can buy your wedding dress there, get your dentures fixed or trade in your old barbecue. It is an exciting urban wonder that I love and rely upon.

The workers' huts at the future Fyshwick were luxurious compared to the more rustic conditions in the tent camps. By the time construction began on Hostel Number One, Parliament House and the sewers, thousands of men were staying yearly in a variety of camps stretching from the nascent city's northern tip at Northbourne and across the river to Eastlake, Westlake, the brickworks at Yarralumla and around the foot of Red Hill.

The most populous were at Westlake, where men were segregated according to their skills.

The tradesmen's camps and those for married skilled men were distinct and more comfortable than the 'Pug' (horse and dray) camps and those for the lowest – the unskilled labourers. Each was informally but quite rigidly segregated on social lines. It was rare for the inhabitants of one camp to mix with those of another.

The labourers' camps were magnets for vagrants, blackmarket liquor salesmen and itinerant Aboriginals – especially on pay days when two-up games proliferated. Prostitutes, naturally, worked them. Those who lived in the marrieds' camps forbade children from going near the labourers' camps.

Many workers were veterans who, having fought at Gallipoli, Palestine or on the Western Front, were returning to pre-war trades. Others – skilled or unskilled – belonged to a vast tribe of lost Australian men suffering 'shell shock' or whose maladies were defined as 'NYD' – Not Yet Diagnosed. Some had untreated venereal disease – a curse on the Western Front and Palestine that claimed as many casualties as trench foot and dysentery. They wandered the country as 'swaggies', picking up work here and there. In Canberra they stayed in or about the camps while working.

There were formal attempts to rehabilitate some lost veterans. In 1922, 200 ex-servicemen – considered the more hopeless cases – were chosen to work in Canberra.

After the mud, dust, flies and dysentery of Gallipoli, the Somme and Palestine, the veterans lived sometimes three to a canvas tent in low-lying areas of Canberra at Eastlake, Westlake or Causeway. While winter was not quite as muddy as on the European front or summer as baking and fly-blown as those under blinding Palestinian skies, life at the camps was appalling and ugly. Hundreds of shell-shocked single men lived in conditions that must have been eerily resonant of those they endured on the frontlines where their traumas began. The Returned Sailors and Soldiers Imperial League of Australia was active in early Canberra. But support for single veterans, especially the injured and maimed, often amounted to little more than keeping them off the streets and finding them rudimentary employment where possible. For the most part the lot of the veteran in Canberra was one of endurance – of the harsh physical conditions that could only have compounded their haunting memories of unspeakable fear, of lost mates and killing.

The conditions for many of the labourers, the veterans included (no blankets provided; poor food; fifteen men to one grubby bathtub), combined with the loneliness and the grog to take a heavy toll and to create an intimidating, malevolent atmosphere, especially after dark. A number of coroner's cases indicated that relatively young men died of alcohol poisoning and organ failure resulting from heavy drinking. Others, like veteran Charles Bruce, died after falling when drunk (his mates paid for a coffin and buried him in an unmarked plot at St John's). Others perished in fires that engulfed tents when lamps were accidentally pushed over or men fell asleep smoking.

The capital's first policeman, Sergeant Philip Cook, recalled plenty of fights.

Alcohol was invariably the cause.

In 1927 Charles Goodrich was acquitted of killing his best mate John Miley at Westlake Labourers' Camp. Both were veterans.

It began much as any other night at Westlake according to a report in *The Canberra Times* on 13 January 1927.

'I went to the tent occupied by Jackie Walker. When I arrived there Walker and a man named Ted were there. Jackie Walker asked me to have a drink of whisky, which I had, and went to my own tent … I wrote a letter and about half an hour later I returned to Walker's tent,' said Goodrich, a father of five from Balmain.

> The same two men were there then. After having the whiskey I decided to return the drink and asked Nimitybelle, who was going into town by car, to bring me back four or five bottles of beer and I gave him 10/-. When Nimitybelle came back he said he had forgotten the beer and handed me a bottle of wine instead, which I accepted. Walker, Ted, Nimity and myself finished the bottle of wine; a chap they called 'Julia Grey' came into the

> tent with more beer and wine – about two bottles of wine and four or five bottles of beer. We were drinking and two more chaps came in …

So it continued until Walker smashed a beer bottle on Goodrich's head. Goodrich stumbled back to his own tent, where he retrieved a long knife – by the sounds of it a First Australian Imperial Force bayonet. He returned looking for Walker. Blinded by his blood, he accidentally stabbed Miley in the head.

Miley and Goodrich were taken to hospital at Acton. Before he died, Miley told police he wanted no action taken against his friend. A jury believed Goodrich's account and acquitted him of manslaughter.

Sergeant Cook said sly grog was probably the biggest problem. In an interview with the Melbourne *Argus* on 26 March 1938 he said:

> I was once asked to give an estimate of the amount of liquor consumed on the territory. That was a pretty tough question. Strange to say, just about that time the first bottle-oh arrived on the scene and helped me with my estimate. The man had seen his opportunities – they were stacked in huge piles

> in various parts of he camp; not little heaps but real stacks. He got busy with chaffbags. He collected 170,000 dozen bottles – or 2,040,000 single bottles – and sent them by special train to Sydney.

Even had the men who worked on Canberra's building sites been able to afford the more expensive accommodation, the Federal Capital Commission – which administered the territory from 1925 to 1930 – would not permit them to stay there.

The camps had their own social strata. But division between the camps and the rest of developing Canberra society in the suburbs of Reid, Blandfordia, Griffith, Manuka and Red Hill was pronounced.

Canberra Illustrated asked:

> Will Canberra some day be known as the city of snobs? At the present the signs are here. First we have the 'guests' at the Hotel Canberra, then the denizens of Acton and so on through Blandfordia, Eastlake, Westlake, the Hotel Ainslie (Gorman House) down to the Causeway and Molonglo and the tradesmens' messes until we finally reach the labourers' camps at Eastlake and Civic Centre, and the home of the lost and outcast [Westlake].

The workers' camps were eventually abandoned. But two, Westlake and Causeway, became permanent suburbs after close and socially coherent communities grew from the simple 'portable' wooden cottages that were erected there for the married men in the 1920s. The lake, a design centrepiece of Griffin's plan with its water and land axes, might well have been part of a planned city in some parallel universe – so distant a reality had it come to seem. Proof of how seriously the early planners, federal politicians and residents took the proposed lake could be found in the Royal Canberra Golf Course, the Acton Race Course and the sporting fields (cleared of livestock before football matches) that had become established in the proposed western basin. For the second generation of public service families and for those communities such as Westlake and Causeway that had evolved from the workers' camps, Canberra's ornamental waters were viewed, in practical terms, as ever distant.

For decades, amid continuing haranguing from the press about the cost to taxpayers of the capital, the planners and the successive governments they served had endlessly delayed the lake – although a version of it (less sculpted than Griffin's original and without his elaborate series of weirs, but serving the all-important axes nonetheless) always remained on 'the plan'. In the end, Menzies, who took up the Canberra cause during his second prime ministership in the 1950s, insisted on the lake and funded it.

Westlake's homes had all been removed by the 1960s. By April 1964 the lower levels of Westlake – including the sites of the labourers' camps – had flooded. Menzies officially opened Lake Burley Griffin in October 1964.

But Causeway, ignored since its inception by the rest of socially conscious Canberra, refused to die. Its rundown cottages were replaced in the 1960s and 70s by simple brick houses, largely the domain of public tenants. Initially Causeway existed to service the rickety railway bridge or 'causeway' over the Molonglo. A great flood in 1922 washed the bridge away. But it has continued to grow as a workers' suburb. In Canberra then, as of recent decades, Causeway – reputedly with its pram-pushing teenagers, its abandoned cars, its shabby houses, drug problem and high unemployment rate – is rarely thought of. That is because, crammed in behind the railway station at Kingston and the Molonglo wetlands, the rest of Canberra rarely sees it.

Right through the 50s, 60s and even the 70s, Causeway was famous for the strong, almost defiant, sense of community that set it apart from the rest of Canberra. Causeway's community ethos was always rooted in the proud self-awareness of residents that they were viewed as socially and economically inferior by 'old' or establishment Canberra whose streets began a few hundred metres away. Causeway's optimism that life could only get better there is encapsulated in a simple weatherboard hall. Conceived by the Canberra Social Service Association (a creation of the Federal Capital Commission and intended to engender community spirit and gauge social need) as a communal space for workers, the men erected Causeway Hall in a day in 1925. It is an understated, modest building. With its simple stage, ticket box, peaked roof, bench seats, wooden floors and upstairs projection room, this place would host dancing, public meetings, movies, visiting thespians and magicians and, of course, musical recitals.

After the more ambitious and expansive Albert Hall opened in 1928, Causeway Hall became a second venue for Canberra's events. But it remained the heart of Causeway.

Frank Moorhouse's Campbell Berry ventured into Causeway Hall in the 1950s. Amid the hysteria of Petrov and fears about Soviet infiltration of Labor's left and the unions, Menzies is planning to ban the Communist Party of Australia. Berry attends a meeting of supporters and members of the party protesting against the proposed ban. Janice, the girlfriend of her brother, is chaperoning Berry.

Janice says: 'I haven't prepared you for the causeway ... The Causeway hall is just a leftover from pre-war Canberra. It's a little forgotten village of workers who live there – was a workers' camp. It'll be demolished.'

Today, there are no signs pointing to what little remains of Causeway. But I know where it is, having dropped my son at the birthday party years ago of a primary school classmate. Only three streets of grim, dilapidated brick houses remain. The burgeoning Kingston Foreshore development of medium-rise architect-designed apartments, with communal outdoor space, is fast swallowing Causeway. Its residents will, Canberra has been assured, be moved to 'appropriate' accommodation. The foreshore will include a small public housing component; the luckier among them will live there. Few outside Causeway will care that it will all, except the hall, be demolished, its people dispersed and its proud community lost.

Causeway has always been a 'forgotten little village', I think, as I walk around near the hall. The weeds out front have grown long. The footpath is covered with smashed glass. A line of shopping trolleys stands next to the hall. I count three derelict cars in the streets.

Two kids in green Raiders guernseys, one a teenager, the other younger, stop and watch.

'Cop,' says one.

Outsiders – which is to say, anyone from elsewhere in Canberra – have never really been welcome in Causeway.

From Causeway I go looking for clues of the existence of Westlake or of the temporary workers' camps it replaced. I leave the car down by the boat-launching area not far from the Yarralumla Yacht Club by the lake and contemplate a steady stream of lycra-wearing cyclists tearing along the path beside Alexandrina Drive. They're not like urban cyclists in most cities. They are dressed for the Tour de France, not the commute. Cycling around the lake's extensive network of paths is a great recreation here. But unless you live in the older original suburbs where the streets are quieter and it's possible to find a rat-run between the major avenues, it is not a great means of transport.

Neither is commuting by foot. Footpaths are rare in parts. So parents pushing prams or kids riding bicycles, skateboards and scooters have to do so on the road. Public transport is lousy. Griffin's trams never eventuated, although thanks to his foresight, the avenues still have space for them. It will cost the best part of a billion dollars to link Civic to Gungahlin by light rail. It will probably never happen. Meanwhile, we've still got the bus – which I have vowed I will catch once before I've lived here twenty years. Canberra belongs to the car.

I chance a gap between cycling mobs and cross Alexandrina Drive. To my left is a construction site surrounded by high Colorbond walls topped by razor wire – a curious level of security. I later discover it is the site of the new Chinese Embassy. China already has such a significant presence a few hundred metres from here – a theme park-style monolith just outside the Parliamentary Triangle near the British High Commission and the Hyatt's croquet lawn. Members of the Falun Gong religion, banned and persecuted in China, mount a daily vigil outside the embassy. The Chinese spies watch them. ASIO, meanwhile, watches the Chinese.

The Chinese have not been easily overlooked here in recent decades. When the current embassy was built in the early 1990s, ASIO wired listening devices into the mortar. The place has been alive with 'bugs' ever since. Perhaps that accounts for the security at the new embassy. Beijing's growing presence in this highly symbolic part of the city seems an appropriate, if unwelcome, reflection of Australia's international diplomatic, defence and trade priorities. If, as many suggest, the Parliamentary Triangle is the face of Australian democracy, then China is a deep furrow in the brow.

I trek up past the construction site and bush bash along the top of a ridge. It's heavy-going through prickly shrubs. After about 400 metres I descend and cross a small dry creek bed. An autumnal pre-dusk milky aura highlights the copses of yellow box redgums. The air is still but for thousands of tiny winged insects that are highlighted in the luminescence like moths in a projector's beam.

I wander along the ridge and down, where signs of old Westlake are all around: painted white rocks that bordered a veggie patch; a few shattered Canberra reds from an outhouse; slivers of foggy old bottle; a lone, struggling rose bush from a once-proud front garden; part of a rotting wooden gate post; rusty hinges and bolts.

Long before Westlake this was a corroboree ground. Some trees still bear Aboriginal markings. There are also trees that were sacred and superstitious for the Scots of Westlake: a rowan and a hawthorn planted to ward off evil. Scotland was always close to Westlake's heart. A chapter of the Burns Club opened here in the late 1920s.

But memories of this place are dying out now. Recalled one old resident:

> Those of us who return to walk where houses and tents once stood see not just a park, but a world as it was in our time. Over there is the tree I climbed and there my dog Toby is buried. On that spot was Dixon's house which burnt down and see that tree at the side of the hall – I played softball there with the other kids.

The kids walked to and from school across paddocks, sodden in winter and dusty in summer. Beneath the old trees two men recline against small backpacks, drinking beer from long-necked bottles. A small circle of rocks holds the charcoal of last night's fire. They appear overdressed for such a warm afternoon, in fleeces and beanies. But then I see their sleeping bags draped over a nearby fallen log. The autumn evenings are cold. Using the remnants of last year's wood stock, I've already lit my open fire for the first time this year.

They see me. One stands, faces me and puts his hands on his hips territorially. I gesture – half salute, half wave – and take a step or two closer. Then a grey and white dog, part work animal and part bull terrier, with a muscular chest, huge swinging balls and a thick silver chain around its neck, materialises at his heels. The dog emits a baritone growl.

I subtly, slowly, change direction. The dog bounds over. I stop, keep my hands up while it sniffs my feet and bare shins, thankful my dog is not here; this one would make a quick snack of her.

The guy waits until his dog is done sniffing. Then whistles. The animal returns and sits at his feet, poised for an order.

'Nice dog,' I say.

'Thanks.'

'Staffy.'

'Cross, heeler.'

'Camping out,' I say. 'Nice night for it.'

'There's other places. But they won't take dogs.'

'Don't blame you.'

'Drink?' he asks, extending the bottle.

'Not tonight – gotta get the kids.'

'Right. See you then.'

'Night.'

I walk briskly back towards the lake, cross the road and head over to where one of the main workers' camps once stood.

The lake shimmers gunmetal grey. The crisp, full sails of the little yachts shoot across the surface, slashing at the multi-coloured background visage of the National Museum at Acton like small white daggers. Dragon-boaters chant their rugger bugger incantations and laugh as they push off from the bank, while families wander over to the yacht club for fish and chips on the lawns before the lake. Between the club and Lotus Bay there's a little rise, covered in oaks and poplars – their leaves a vivid yellow carpet beneath.

I kick about the crushed acorns and leaves, and

push aside an empty condom wrapper, cigarette butts and two syringes. A few centimetres later the earth gives up some nails, what looks like the blade of a small pocketknife and part of a fountain pen. Much of this camp lies out there, on the bottom of the lake.

How disappointing that lake was when they first dammed the Molonglo in 1963. It was one of the parched years when the exotics in the front yards at Forrest, Griffith, Reid and Deakin shriveled, when Weston's roses wilted and Lake George was covered with grazing sheep. Lake Burley Griffin turned into a fetid swamp, heavy on the nose and a mosquito breeding ground. And then the rains came in 1964 and Menzies could finally declare it open.

The hardships, loneliness, the blood and booze of the camps washed away with the flooding of the Molonglo Valley. As Canberra dismantled the unsightly huts that formed the village of Westlake, it cleansed itself of the workers' camps. Almost.

Plasterer Walter Sheen worked on Parliament House for eleven years.

He later wrote about how, after arriving at one of the earliest workers' camps, the foreman arranged his accommodation.

> … he took me outside to a hut, which was to be my quarters. Then the carpenter arrived + was told to make me a stretcher which he did, after making the stretcher he put nails each side of it. Then he said we will get three chaff bags + a sugar bag …+ the bags were filled with leaves, these he said will be your mattress and pillows. He then got two more bags + said have you got a blanket. I said yes, he then fastened the chaff bags on to the side of the stretcher and said when you get into bed, pull the chaff bag over the blanket and fasten it on to the nail on the opposite side, because if you don't + you happen to fall out of bed, you will freeze to death.

Sheen later raised his family at Westlake.

He recalled with particular pride one plastering job at Parliament House:

> Strange to say that the Coat of Arms on Parliament House was incorrect. Both heads were facing in the same direction, which caused much

> embarrassment to the Gov members ... The Kangaroos head was cut + turned to face the Emu. A new jaw, ear + eyes had to be moulded, then it was found that the heads were at a wrong distance from the centre star. To correct this I had to cut the emu's neck at the bottom + remodel the neck. Which proved a success + when Mr Bronoski [senior parliamentary official Robert Broinowski] came to look at it he was delighted with the job. He said stay here Mr Sheen + he went down + took 14 members out to the front of Par House. One of the members beckoned to me to go down which I did + he said [to] me, you haven't finished the job yet go back + make a pouch on the kangaroo + put a little joey looking out. They were all delighted with the job I had made.

I am looking up at the Australian and the British coats of arms. There are a few tourists waiting to go into the Museum of Australian Democracy, as the old house is today. They look at me strangely because I look strange.

I've found the tell-tale signs of Sheen's handiwork. There, just above the kangaroo's right shoulder is a barely discernible scar, just under the grey enamel paint of the 'roo's pelt, where he wielded the hacksaw blade. It's also evident where the emu's neck has been cut from the nape through to the lower breast so its head could also be turned around to face the kangaroo's.

Then I inspect the steps down which I had, as a six-year-old, watched Whitlam bound.

I'm looking for chips in the stonework, preferably hoove-shaped, that, I'm assured, were made in 1979.

That was when Roger McDonald launched his novel, *1915*, about a group of young Australian men from the bush who served in World War I. Some of his mates, horsemen from around Bungendore, added to the festivities with a display of tent-pegging on the lawns out front. McDonald said:

> The idea came up to dress up the Bungendore B polo team as light horsemen. Where we got the uniforms from and so on I can't remember. There must have been some sort of historical reconstruction society or something. And then tent-pegging, you know, riding with a sword and then leaning down from your saddle and sticking out a tent peg from the ground was a kind of equestrian sport. I don't know that they'd done it before – they probably hadn't, but they practised

> it and they got to do it reasonably well. And so they did a tent pegging demonstration in the area between the Parliament House and the National Library.
>
> And then after the launch was over and they all had a few wines, a couple of them rode up to the steps of Parliament House – they took their horses up the steps intending to go right through the front doors. And that's where the security people told them to back off. And they later sent me a bill for damage to the steps – about $40.

I go inside to meet Libby Stewart, a historian at the museum who, like me, waits for a day when Canberra residents become genuinely oblivious to the criticisms of the rest of Australia. It won't, I'm sure, have happened by the time the city turns a hundred on 12 March 2013.

> Getting over that is part of the maturing process. And I think that's got a way to go. Definitely. I mean as locals we raise kids here and we live here and we know what a great city it is. But it's like Australia and the cultural cringe generally – when we stop having to tell people what a great place it is then we will be mature.

We are sitting in Stewart's office on the first floor of the labyrinthine old Parliament. I've always found the place unfriendly and oppressive, in contrast with those who worked there before moving to the new Parliament House up on Capital Hill in 1988, who insist the later building is sterile, soulless and hostile to human interaction.

There's a pile of T-shirts and stickers on Stewart's desk. They are emblazoned with slogans calling for an ELECTION NOW and NO CARBON TAX. A few weeks earlier Stewart and her colleagues had walked up the gentle rise to grassy Federation Mall – the designated 'protest area' outside Parliament House. They bought the stickers from members of the so-called 'Convoy of no confidence' – a disparate and angry bunch of malcontents whose protest hinged on a threatened truckers' 'blockade' of Parliament House that failed to materialise, as they milled around the mall, calling the prime minister a bitch and a witch and demanding an election.

The T-shirts and stickers contribute to the museum's growing collection of political ephemera. Future visitors will be able to learn about the divisive carbon tax by means of the items, in the same way as they will learn about Australia's anti-

Vietnam, land rights and suffragette movements from the banners, posters, flyers and protest buttons in the collection.

At the convoy protest, Mick Pattel, a Queensland truck driver and president of the National Road Freighters Association, was reported as saying: 'It's unfortunate for the people of Canberra that the Parliament is sitting right in the middle of their city and while we certainly don't want to hurt the people of Canberra, the politicians who live there are hurting us.'

It made me angry.

In a newspaper column a few days later, I wrote: 'Hey Mick, news flash: the federal politicians don't live in Canberra. They just happen to come here for a few nights a week for less than half of the year. But they do have electoral offices and there's one near you. Why not take your truck and park it out front there?'

I read my column the day it was printed in the paper. I cringed. Had I become one of the glass-jawed Canberra NIMBYs I have always abhorred? Like those who regularly ring in to a segment called *Chief Minister Talk Back* on the local ABC radio station to complain about the ACT's ban on plastic shopping bags or the potholes or the exorbitant price of parking ($8 a day!) or the colour of the paint on the signs of the Gungahlin Drive Extension and, while they're at it, about the time it took to come in on the GDE this morning.

Why do I care what this guy says? It's been that way since Parliament House opened in 1927, about which I'm talking to Libby Stewart.

She says there was great excitement nationally that the Duke of York (later George VI) and the Duchess of York, Elizabeth, were to attend the opening. Dame Nellie Melba was also expected to pull crowds.

Tens of thousands of spectators were expected for the opening on 9 May 1927. Official guests filled the territory's few guesthouses and the Hotel Canberra. If the punters wanted to come they'd have to camp. The authorities clearly thought the place would be overrun. They catered accordingly with truckloads of fresh seafood and Sergents meat pies and sausage rolls from Sydney.

The Duke, afflicted with a crippling stutter that made public appearance an anxious affair, secretly visited Parliament House the evening before to practise his speech.

Stewart explains:

> There was a lot of hype. And perhaps the event didn't quite live up to that. They were expecting many tens of thousands of people to come. But when you think about it Canberra was quite a difficult place to get to – you know, a dodgy train line from Sydney and not very good roads and no accommodation … the reality is they just didn't come. They knew beforehand that there was nowhere to stay, so they just didn't come in those sorts of numbers.

It had been hoped the horse-drawn carriage taking the Duke and Duchess from Yarralumla (by then, acquired as the vice-regal residence) would glide through streets ten-deep with spectators. The roads were near empty.

And what about the wasted pies that Dad said became the foundation of a public service building?

> There was this farcical situation of the catering … they brought down trucks and trucks of food and of course it was all wasted. Rumours started that the leftover food was taken to a nearby place which later turned into an administration building … now the John Gorton Building, and Finance I think is now in that building, and that it supposedly

> formed the foundations of the building. As far as we can tell, that didn't happen. The food ended up at Queanbeyan. Because Queanbeyan had a tip. Ten thousand odd pies, sausage rolls, cooked prawns and fish – all buried in landfill.

The fledgling Royal Australian Air Force had ordered twenty aircraft to continually circle the hills around the Limestone Plains and pass over Parliament House. The noise was deafening.

The Sydney Morning Herald of 10 May 1927 reported: 'The message from the King was read by the Duke of York in clear and measured tones that gave full force to the words. Even the slight hesitation which came very rarely rather heightened the effort …'

But according to Melbourne's *The Argus* – a Canberra skeptic – on 10 May 1927, the Duke's pervasive anxiety might well have been misplaced.

' …unfortunately the speeches of [Prime Minister] Mr Bruce and the Duke of York, like the singing of Dame Nellie Melba, suffered through the sound being drowned by the roar of the aeroplanes that were circling overhead.'

Melba, it is said, was already somewhat unimpressed with arrangements; an official had slipped a newspaper under her feet after she'd complained about standing on the bare, cold concrete.

A memorial stone in the yard at St John's indicates what happened next:

> In Loving Memory
> of
> FLYING OFFICER
> F.C. EWEN R.A.A.F.
> WHO CRASHED AT CANBERRA
> MAY 9TH 1927
> LATE N.Z.S.C. S/C – R.M.C.
> DUNTROON
> BELOVED SON OF F.C. & L. EWEN
> BORN KAMO NEW ZEALAND
> AGED 28 YEARS

The *Herald* reported: 'The happiness and rejoicing at Canberra today were marred by a fatal aeroplane accident which occurred in full view of the many thousands who had gathered on the parade ground to witness the review.'

The accident, never adequately explained, was later described by the coroner as 'one of those inexplicable happenings, the secret of which died with the pilot'.

Apparently while flying in formation just north-west of Parliament House, Ewen's plane dived sharply from a height of some 500 feet and crashed roughly where the National Library of Australia stands today.

Ewen survived the impact, but with terrible injuries, including broken legs and arms. He died that night.

The accident shocked the Duke, himself a pilot.

It was an inauspicious end to a day that had already failed to meet great expectations.

The Great Depression ended Canberra's short post-war growth spurt.

The workers were sacked and the camps – where some had lived under canvas for years – closed.

The Depression's aftermath concertinaed with World War II, effectively leaving Canberra behind until the 1950s. A skeleton camp remained open at Mount Ainslie for itinerant workers. The men who were sacked – including many damaged World War I veterans for whom building the capital had offered a semblance of stability – found it impossible to secure other work. Some loitered, knocking on front doors seeking odd jobs or charity.

Before the downturn there had been a final burst of building: hostels for single public servants at Brassey House, the Hotel Acton and Hotel Ainslie, and Albert Hall – the building that probably contributed more to the evolving community soul of the capital than any other.

Today, the big conifers largely obscure the fawn-coloured hall from the road. But this architecturally elaborate Georgian Revival building, with its grand arched French windows of Queensland maple and expansive interior, has a prominent place on Commonwealth Avenue close to the apex of the land axis at Capital Hill, befitting its intended importance in the cultural and civic life of both Canberra and Australia.

The hall's name was chosen from hundreds the public put forward, reflecting the Duke of York's association with Canberra years before. It also evoked the art and musical culture of London's own venue of the same name.

Prime Minister Bruce, who opened Albert Hall, hoped the building would be a defining step towards Canberra becoming the centre of Australian art and literature 'and of everything that will uplift the Australian people – a centre from which we will radiate all those aspirations that are truly national'.

Albert Hall did become Canberra's cultural and civic heart for the best part of thirty-five years. Barely a month after the hall opened (memorably, the velvet curtains caught fire at the ceremony on 10 March 1928), it hosted its first balls. Canberra's first Anzac Day ceremony took place there in the same year and in June it hosted the second National Assembly of Rotary International. St Gabriel's, the predecessor to the Church of England Girl's Grammar School, held its first mid-winter ball there a week later.

A state-of-the-art German projector enabled it to be used as a cinema (competition for the Capitol Theatre, Manuka's striking Deco landmark) and, until the opening of the Canberra Theatre in 1965, it was the only venue capable of accommodating up to 700 people. It was the stage of public protests (anti-taxation in 1928), hearings (the Constitutional Royal Commission in 1930), plays (Clemence Dane's controversial *A Bill of Divorcement* in 1932) and public speakers (H.G. Wells in 1938, after which he joined community firefighters in tackling a bushfire on Black Mountain). In August

1945 the Albert Hall was the beacon for an isolated community eager to celebrate war's end; hundreds gathered, impromptu, to dance, to drink, to kiss. They formed a conga line through the hall, out the doors, and around the outside. For all the decades before Canberra won self-government, Albert Hall was the venue for town-hall style public and committee meetings about civic, social and planning issues that affected residents.

Albert Hall also hosted Australia's first citizenship ceremonies for post-war European migrants in the 1950s.

I have driven past the building thousands of times. But I've never before been inside, having filed the Albert Hall away in my consciousness as a rather forgotten and sadly pretentious place – a recent venue for sales of exotic floor coverings, antiques and ski gear. It was also the venue, before my time in Canberra, for the now legendary wedding party of my friends, Marcus Kelson and Virginia Cook, and for many emerging Canberra bands in the 1970s and 80s.

Out the front I meet Lenore Coltheart, a prominent historian of Canberra, a biographer of the Australian-born suffragette Jessie Street and the historical consultant on Moorhouse's *Cold Light*.

Like many school children of the late 1940s and 50s, Coltheart – a Canberra High School student – attended her share of speech nights and dances at Albert Hall. She says:

> The Albert Hall … reflects and speaks of and sings to us about the glue that holds us together. It also reminds us of the aspirations at the beginning of the century, about what kind of nation Australia could be. Putting the new Parliament House where Griffin wanted a Capitol building – a peoples' building – and then calling it the Capital rather than Capitol represents a huge change from what the aspirations were for the Griffin ideal. Old Parliament House embodies it and so does Albert Hall. They're twins. The Old House embodies the legislative part of it and this embodies the civic part of it.

We climb the steep staircase to the old projector room, dusty and covered with discarded papers. Canisters of reel-to-reel film litter the floor. She points out that Albert Hall was where post-colonial organisations – including the associations of librarians and planners – decided to federate, and the venue for Australia's first national art exhibitions.

We go backstage, which smells of damp and mice. The orchestra pit is filled with chairs. The stage is bisected by a large Compton Theatre Organ, the size of a ute, restored in the 1980s by the local chapter of the ACT Theatre Organ Association. Why there? Well, it had to go somewhere. The place is in sad disrepair. Australia has forgotten its Albert Hall, a building as essential to Canberra's cultural heritage as Old Parliament House.

We stand in the balcony between stalls of fold-down seats, their brown leather cracked and split, and look down on the sprung dance floor – just like the long-gone mums who watched, like the Red Hill eagles, their daughters and their consorts below.

Coltheart sees Albert Hall as a metaphor for the way Australia views its capital.

> Well, where else but Canberra is the national symbolism? Other capital cities have town halls … We often refer to it as Canberra's town hall because it performs those functions. But it performed them for Australia, too. But the less Canberra is thought of as the national capital, the less the national capital we become and really this symbolises that decline, you know.

The federal government doesn't want it and the local authorities can't think what to do with it, she says.

Just like poor *Bellona,* the bronze statue of the Goddess of War who stared defiantly down from her plinth daring the politicians to display her somewhere – anywhere. The renowned European-based, Australian-born sculptor Bertram Mackennal, who for a brief time in 1883 worked with Rodin, cast *Bellona* in 1906. She didn't sell. So he gave her to the federal government in 1916 as a tribute to the Australians dying in the war.

She arrived at Parliament House, Melbourne, in 1921. Prime Minister Billy Hughes dispatched her to the basement. Then came a brainstorm: as a sculpture about war, she clearly belonged at the Australian War Memorial that was being planned for Canberra. The only problem was that the memorial would not open until 1941. *Bellona* would need a home in the meantime.

So they plonked her (minus Mackennal's marble pedestal) on a dusty piece of ground between two lanes of Commonwealth Avenue outside Albert Hall.

Her great iron helmet bearing the unsettling visage of her brother Mars, and with her perky bosoms bared, *Bellona* glowered from a utilitarian concrete stand at the Molonglo. An odd fit, but she was Canberra's first statue and the people, then as now, neither uptight nor prudish, emotionally embraced their fellow import. In October 1933 locals driving across the Molonglo couldn't help but notice the bra that she was suddenly wearing. In March 1939 pranksters leant *Bellona* some modesty with a pair of conical breast shields fashioned from melted gramophone records. In 1954 there was general community anger when vandals applied red paint to her offending bits. Queen Elizabeth II was about to arrive in Canberra to open the twenty-fifth Parliament; police regarded *Bellona* as an unwanted distraction. About a day before the Queen was set to arrive, *Bellona* was found wearing an oversized pink bra.

Someone then covered her in green paint. She was promptly removed. After the Queen's visit, a large professionally cut tombstone appeared where *Bellona* had stood: 'R.I.P. Goddess Bellona.'

The war memorial didn't much want *Bellona*. So she ended up in the memorial's basement before being moved to territory administration storage huts in Parkes – the same place Marion Mahony Griffin's beautiful but unwanted renderings of

Canberra ended up a decade earlier. Dame Alexandra Hasluck, the wife of Governor-General Sir Paul Hasluck, put *Bellona* in the grounds of Yarralumla. After a heated internal debate about whether *Bellona* symbolised aggression or sacrifice, the war memorial decided it wanted her back … but not permanently until a sculpture garden was built around a tree propagated from seed taken from those at Gallipoli's Lone Pine. Finally in 1993 *Bellona* was moved yet again – this time she stood directly outside Albert Hall, a few hundred metres from where she was removed in 1954. In 1999, after the Lone Pine had grown sufficiently, *Bellona* moved permanently to the war memorial.

By the late 1920s, Griffin's 'city beautiful' plan for a capital combining grand monuments with medium- and high-density dwelling and communal recreation grounds was lost. In its place was an evolving low-density 'garden city' of cottages and bungalows on big blocks, each screened with trees from the next.

The city's emerging suburbs reflected a stratified society that had taken root in the earliest days of the camps. The workers would live at Westlake, Causeway (by then Kingston) and, if they could afford to, Ainslie and Reid, while higher-ranking public servants would live around Griffith. The senior bureaucrats would have the best blocks – and houses – at Forrest and along the base of Red Hill at Mugga Way.

Ironically, the class distinction in Canberra's housing market derived from the decision at the capital's inception to ensure that all of the federal territory lands remained in Commonwealth ownership. This Griffin had supported because he thought it reflected the equality underpinning federation, and deterred land speculation that would enrich only property developers and investors. Those who 'bought' a house or land in early Canberra were effectively paying 5 per cent annually of the appraised value of the land – or the house on it – for a ninety-nine-year lease. But the Federal Capital Commission unofficially predetermined who would live in which suburbs by fixing block prices and lease covenants that specified minimum building costs. The first auctions for the small workers' estate of Corroboree Park, Ainslie, specified a minimum building cost of £700. In Reid, for mid-ranking public servants it was £1000. At

Blandfordia it was at least £1500, while in Mugga Way the blocks were a minimum of £3500. Calthorp's House, built in 1927, was the first house on Mugga Way.

The Ainslie weatherboards – functional, cheap, practical and with minimum amenities – stood on big blocks. So, too, did the Reid and Kingston cottages (the government printers mostly lived in the latter). Invariably painted white, they stood out on the plains for decades until Weston's carefully spaced trees and hedges took shape. Houses in more sought-after suburbs were built in what became known as the 'FCC Style' – something of a hybrid that borrowed elements from the Mediterranean and the Georgian, and (accidentally) with components that would have been at ease in Griffin's Prairie houses. The single storey, the pitched roof and the low arch – despite its capacity to cast a significant internal shadow and to steal winter sunlight – were favoured. So, too, were small curved roads – the shapes adapted from Griffin's original plan but without deference to his broader widths, communal spaces and zonings – in which houses faced one another with little consideration for light and air.

In 1927 the Melbourne and Sydney Buildings

opened in Civic. For well over a decade these two great white double-storey blocks – with their sweeping Spanish-style arches, deep external walkways, internal courtyards and mixture of commercial and retail businesses – *were* the city. They mirrored each other across the great expanse of Northbourne Avenue that waited then, as today, for a sign of Griffin's tramway down the middle.

In 1940 Eilean Giblin observed of the Melbourne and Sydney Buildings:

> Between them are lawns with trees and seats – Holly trees, red with berries, and various cypresses ... Civic centre is about 4 miles from here [Forrest] and I drove to it by the Prime Minister's Lodge and along State Circuit where no development or building had yet begun ... Civic Centre is also called the City, although I have no idea why this should be, unless indeed it is because all the Banks are collected there, and perhaps banks make a city.

We don't have front fences here. Canberra has always loved a hedge, just as it is utterly enamored of the leaf blower today.

Early residents were encouraged to plant hedges

– and apricot, pear, apple and quince trees. The hedges were frequently inspected and trimmed by workers from the commission and later from the Department of Interior, part of whose function was to cultivate and preserve the streetscapes. They would implore householders to tidy the front yard and where necessary even do it themselves. (The local government today takes responsibility for street trees, although not – as I find myself lamenting – our hedges.) This gave rise to one of the enduring myths about Canberra: residential front gardens were maintained by brigades of lawn-mowing, hedge-trimming public servants.

Journalist and poet Kenneth Slessor was impressed with Canberra's houses. He wrote in his 1966 book *Canberra*:

> The houses of Canberra are almost as great a pleasure as the trees. The city inherited no legacy from the terrace builders of the nineteenth century, no belts of Edwardian frightfulness, no mass-produced slums or tenements, and no twisted thoroughfares. Thus its living quarters, no matter how large or small, princely or modest, have been built to a design from the beginning. No pattern is repeated and each house has its own character.

> There are no nightmares here of the kind familiar to London's Bloomsbury or Camberwell in which part of the surrealist horror is the problem of trying to recognise your home in an endless vista of identical buildings.

(I love Slessor's poetic aside, later in this piece, that while 'other capitals' were 'accretions of history superimposed on primitive encampments', Canberra was 'a test-tube insemination conducted in a laboratory'.)

In the early 1960s photographer Frank Hurley turned his camera on Canberra for his book, *Canberra: A Camera Study*. Hurley, renowned for his beautifully, elaborately composed – and sometimes staged – photographs of both world wars and Shackleton's polar expedition, clearly found Canberra's order and symmetry alluring. His book features my favourite buildings – the old Anatomy School (probably my favourite Canberra building) at Acton, the magnificently domed Academy of Science, the old Patents Office, the Sydney and Melbourne Buildings, and some of the more representative houses. But there are few people in the shots. Instead, Hurley gave us a display village of topiary precision and seamless concrete render in a gloriously soothing palette to match Canberra's wondrous imported tapestry of urban forest. People, where they occasionally featured, appear as if extras from a movie.

'Whether small or stately, there is universal pride in the house. Good maintenance is evident everywhere and it would be difficult to find a home in which the owner is not striving to outshine his neighbour's garden,' Hurley – or his caption writer – wrote.

Others have been far less laudatory about suburban Canberra.

'Instead of a close-knit community whose ideas about the nation and its government could be conceived and manifested, Canberra developed into a low density suburb of separate individuals carefully detached and screened from each other by planting,' Paul Reid wrote.

'The original intention of the Garden City … had been to combine the best of the Country with the best of the Town. Canberra was getting all country and no Town. Nobody objected to living in a garden suburb. But there were consequences such as poor transport, isolation and lack of amenities …'

A reallocation of the public service to bolster the war effort (the war economy was managed by Eilean Giblin's husband, Lyndhurst Falkiner Giblin, chairman of the Commonwealth Financial and Economic Committee), shortages and rationing meant that the development of Canberra became a minor – or non- – priority. The population dwindled. The place became a skeleton city that, while still home to the Parliament, the prime minister and some of the main departments, seemed geographically and emotionally remote from the main state capitals – especially Melbourne, host to Australian defence headquarters until 1961.

The Commonwealth Department of the Interior ('whose interior?' asked Giblin!) oversaw administration of Canberra during the war years. When not searching to the outer reaches of the capital territory for clay for her pottery, Giblin wandered about stunted wartime Canberra scrupulously observing its inhabitants, celebrating its seasons, its flora and its fauna.

Giblin's bemusement at the city's bureaucratic dictates are evident. One day in March 1941 she was sitting at the breakfast table with *The Canberra Times* when a man at the door disturbed her.

> 'I am from the Department.' 'What are you going to do?' I asked. 'Tidy up round the back,' he said, 'if it got dry, all that (and he waved his hand round) might catch fire. It is not safe. And we will tidy up the wattle in the front.' 'We want to cut that down,' I said. 'Have you written to the Department of the Interior about it?' 'No,' I said. I returned to my coffee and *The Canberra Times*, and a few minutes later there was a ring at the front door, and I found a man who said he had come to fix the telephone. I showed him where it was to go … and I returned to coffee and the horrors of the *Times*. Five or ten minutes went by when there was a knock at the back door, and a man said, 'I have brought 2 electric light globes from the Department.'

She wrote about the constant call for blackouts against Japanese planes that ventured inland, food shortages, and rationing of petrol. And she wrote constantly about how frustratingly quiet and inert the city seemed.

> Yesterday afternoon I arrived here, after spending a week in Melbourne where there was noise and strain and worry with some very pleasant

> interludes. Canberra in contrast gives me the impression of emptyness. I walked this morning to the Manuka shops … and saw no one else going, or returning. Emptyness and silence, broken occasionally by a magpie calling, or a dog barking.

During her husband's frequent absences, Giblin remained in Canberra alone, using the solitude to pursue her literary and artistic interests and to consider how the city might grow after the war.

> … I passed St John's Church, which existed before Canberra became the Australian Capital, and then turned to the right and crossed the low paddocks which border the Molonglo whose banks are clustered with weeping willows, very green and graceful at this time of the year. The river was low as there has been little rain for weeks. Canberra is divided into two portions by this river and a stretch of paddocks at times are flooded, and here many sheep and lambs grazed. At some future time I believe the Molonglo is to be dammed and this low-lying part flooded to make a lake. And then there will be no sheep and lambs grazing in the centre of Canberra.

Canberra, as the centre of government, was an obvious target for the Japanese. But its isolation and stultifying quietness that comes through in Giblin's writing, makes such a threat seem incongruous.

She writes how a neighbour asked her 'what are you doing about a [bomb] shelter?'

'Nothing,' I said ... 'What would you do if there was a raid?' Mrs E said. 'Stay in bed,' I replied ... it is difficult to imagine that bombs may actually fall here in Canberra.'

She points to a melancholy among the women who were left alone to keep house, recounting how a neighbour asked how she was liking Canberra.

'In some ways I like it very much,' Giblin said.

'It's a dull place,' she said, 'but it is pretty. Oh if only there were trams passing, how I would like to jump on a tram and go shopping ...'

She wrote about having walked with a young Englishwoman, Mrs Green, married to a diplomat.

> We walked away together as the low afternoon sun was shining on the hills by Queanbeyan and we both agreed that Canberra is a lovely place. But, Mrs Green said, so many of the women are disconnected. They come here having made up

> their minds that they are not going to like it – and they won't like it, she said.

With the exception of the Australian War Memorial, which opened in 1941, there was little significant construction.

Roger McDonald, who lived as a child with his family at Bribbaree and later Temora – both to the north-west of Canberra – recalls visiting the capital on holiday in late 1949.

'We'd camped at Black Mountain – there was a camping ground roughly where the shoreline of the lake is now, behind the ANU [Australian National University] or it could even be underwater. It was long before the lake was filled,' he says.

> I recall this sense as a kid of the place as being these monuments in the grass. There was this great big dry grassy area in summer and at one end of it was the war memorial and at the other end of it was Parliament House and across in behind that somewhere was the Capitol Theatre at Manuka which was like something out of ancient Athens, with all its columns and so on. They are the three things that I remember apart from camping, and then swimming out at the Cotter River.

Swimming in the Cotter (and camping near it) remains a Canberra institution, on par with bathing at the stunning Deco Manuka pool, with its tiled walls, concertinaed wooden benches for sunbaking and the semi-private anterooms at the end where generations of teenagers have canoodled and made secrets since the building, constructed by veterans, opened on Australia Day 1931.

It is a golden autumn day. I start it by walking up the middle of Anzac Parade towards the war memorial. The memorial clings to the base of a mountain appropriately named after Captain James Ainslie – the Canberra pioneer and purported warrior whose legend, possibly erroneously, has him hunted down and wounded grievously by Napoleon's cavalrymen at Waterloo.

The memorial stands as the northern point of Griffin's land axis, which runs from Parliament House at Capital Hill. Before bisecting the lake, the land axis precisely incorporates that odd six-sided foundation stone that O'Malley, Fisher and Lord Denman laid with their golden trowels on 12 March 1913. Then, on the northern bank of the lake, the line continues through Gallipoli Reach (marked by a plaque and a gnarly willow tree). It then cuts across Parkes Way and Constitution Avenue.

Griffin had envisaged Constitution Avenue linking the Australian military headquarters at Russell with Civic along the northern shore of the lake, as a grand boulevard of cosmopolitan charm; a place to stroll, to shop and to gather. Instead, like most of Canberra's avenues, it is a speedway between Russell and Civic for drivers spoilt by pristine multi-lane roads and cheap parking. Some Canberra drivers are among the most aggressive I've struck in the world.

Constitution Avenue was the base of Griffin's Lloyd Wright-style 'pleasance' – the city playground that led to the entertainment precinct, with its beer gardens and casino set amid one of the city's prime residential districts.

Instead, the 'pleasance' became Anzac Parade, in the middle of which I'm standing while trying to reconcile the anomaly between what Griffin imagined and what happened – a 145-metre-wide, six-lane road leading to Australia's most venerable monument. On my far left are the quaint, renovated, heritage-listed cottages of Reid. On the other side are the newer bungalows of Campbell, built in the 1960s, 70s and 80s, with steel and glass and wood.

Great concrete and bronze monuments to the different wars and battles – Vietnam, Korea, Tobruk – and services and corps – Army, Navy, Air Force, mounted – are punctuated with thickets of gums to screen the houses. The median strip where I stand is a parade ground. Granulated red scoria makes a distinct military crunch under my feet as I pass perfectly spaced white boxes filled with the dense, low shrub hebe.

By the time Griffin returned to Australia in May 1914 to oversee capital construction, he'd all but lost his pleasance and entertainment precinct. The declaration of war a few months later killed them.

Today, the competing events that defined Australian nationhood are symbolised on that gun-barrel land axis. On Capital Hill stands the permanent symbol of 1 January 1901 – federation. It is the Mitchell/Giurgola-designed Parliament House, opened in 1988. A few hundred metres down the hill, Canberra is embodied in the foundation stone laid on 12 March 1913. Then comes the open expanse of the lake and, on its northern shore, Gallipoli Reach, which evokes another date

– 25 April 1915 – that has become the most seminal in Australia's cultural evolution. The line ends at the war memorial.

Federation, federal Parliament and the establishment of Canberra – these never stood a chance of defining a national consciousness compared with Gallipoli.

Having witnessed and recorded with painstaking detail and at times unwelcome frankness, the pointless folly of the Gallipoli misadventure that claimed 8141 Australian lives, in 1916 official Australian war correspondent Charles Bean went to the European Western Front. The Western Front hosted a global tragedy, a place where the new machines of industrial killing – the warplane, the tank, the machine gun and the mass-produced, high impact bomb and artillery shell – were pitted against the outmoded tactics of land battle – the trench-launched infantry attack and cavalry charge. The consequences were horrible. Millions died.

From 1914 to 1918, 416 809 Australian men – 39 per cent of the adult male population of the new federation – enlisted to fight; 324 000 of them served overseas; 61 720 died.

About 50 000 Australians died on the Western Front, including some 18 000 who remain unidentified. They were buried in graves marked simply 'An Australian Soldier of the Great War'. Others still lie where they were sucked down into the mud and viscera after dying.

Relatives had little upon which to focus their grief. Very few could visit the battle sites or marked graves. They needed a place in Australia to symbolise their loss and evoke their memories.

From 1916, Bean was determined to establish such a permanent monument, including a military museum and an archive.

From its inception, the memorial inhabited an emotional space similar to the one Griffin had envisioned for his Capitol. The memorial, despite some grumbling in the Melbourne press when it opened, quickly became the place of national pilgrimage. Those who resented Canberra would still visit the memorial, where they could wander the galleries and inspect the dioramas of the places like Lone Pine, Pozières and Romani, that had claimed their men. Future generations could connect with artefacts such as the landing boat that ferried the soldiers to the shores of Anzac Cove in 1915; the beautiful Shellal Mosaic that was looted by the Australian forces under General Sir Harry Chauvel from a Byzantine church in Palestine in 1917; an array of relics from both world wars; and galleries dedicated to Australian involvement in subsequent conflicts, including Korea, Vietnam, Iraq and Afghanistan.

I stop just by the Shellal Mosaic, which has long been fixed to an internal wall at the memorial, prohibiting its future removal. A recent redesign of the Hall of Valour, which honours Australian Victoria Cross winners, has resulted in a partition being set in front of the large window through which the mosaic is viewed. The Australians removed the mosaic piece by piece, before it was sent to Egypt and Australia for 'safekeeping'. I know of at least two families who have inherited tiles from the mosaic; the horsemen who removed it could not avoid the temptation, it seems, to souvenir just a little piece. The new partition looks as if it has been strategically placed to cover up a piece of what is, in reality, war booty.

I wander around the Hall of Valour and read about the VC winners. Where once the stories tended to underestimate the adverse impact of war on the recipients, today they plot more rounded personal stories. And so when we read about Hugo Throssell – the sportsman son of a Western Australian premier, and a light horseman who was traumatised by the death of his brother at Gaza in 1917 – we also learn a little about his struggles after the war. Just beneath his VC medal in a glass display case is Throssell's Webley Mark IV service revolver. The caption reads: 'Haunted by his experiences the Gallipoli hero tragically took his own life after the war. He was found shot, still holding a revolver in his right hand.'

A revolver? It is *the* revolver.

Throssell renounced war after returning to Australia a hero and having married Katharine Susannah Prichard, Bolshevik and novelist. The military establishment ostracised Throssell. His family, who blamed Prichard, disowned and disinherited him. Unemployable, Throssell killed himself so that his wife and son, Ric, could receive his military pension.

Ric Throssell, a playwright and a member of the Department of External Affairs, ultimately lived in Canberra. During the Royal Commission on Espionage (inspired by the Cold War and the defections of the Soviet diplomats Vladimir and Evdokia Petrov), held at Albert Hall in 1954, Throssell was targeted for no other reason than that he was the son of a Bolshevik mother and a war hero who came to be regarded as a traitor.

It was a sad and bitter story that reverberated through the Canberra bureaucracy no less damagingly than the royal commission, and the anti-Communist fear impacted on Evatt's Labor Party, manifesting in The Split.

The Petrovs' home in Griffith – just behind the Russian Embassy and close to the Kingston Hotel – always seems to me to be disproportionately unimposing given the impact its occupants had on Australian public life, not least the Labor Party and, by virtue of that, my family. The place has been painted; the sculpted lavender bushes and the high hedge weren't there in the Petrovs' day. But it's possible to imagine Vlad carefully reversing his Skoda into Lockyer Street after opening the narrow wooden doors of the garage.

In 1983 Ric Throssell gave his father's VC to People for Nuclear Disarmament.

I leave the Hall of Valour and walk briefly into the war memorial's research centre where the archives are available to any Australian. It is where a few years ago I first heard the recorded voices of our soldiers who participated in the massacre of a Palestinian village, Surafend, in December 1918.

Archivists had for years told me that Canberra was the nation's conscience – the keeper of the records that detail Australia for all its good and bad, its courage and cowardice. But only when I heard the crackly recordings of those old mens' raspy voices did I truly understand.

I wander along a hallway lined with images of men who fought: sitting atop a pony ready to face the Boer; lining up in their best clothes to enlist; in a rice paddy in Vietnam; on Kokoda and in Malaya. I pass the landing boat, go outside and stand upstairs on the portico that looks down Anzac Parade. The road is empty of pedestrians. Just behind me is the Tomb of the Unknown Soldier – one of just two Australians who died overseas in World War I whose bodies were returned to Australia.

And this reminds me of the equal significance to Canberra of the other.

On 15 May 1915 a Turkish sniper's bullet severed the femoral artery of Major General William Bridges, commander of the 1st Australian Division at Gallipoli. Bridges had raised the division using as commanding officers his handpicked, drilled and educated graduates from the Royal Military Academy at Duntroon. Bridges was founding commander of the academy. Until the war started, Bridges and his officer cadets were fixtures of Limestone Plains society, including at the Cunningham family's stations at Tuggeranong and Lanyon where they attended dances and dinner parties with the young ladies of the house, and played cricket and tennis.

Bridges died on a hospital ship and was initially buried in Egypt.

Regardless of rank or privilege, Commonwealth policy dictated all men killed would be buried in cemeteries where they died. But pressured by his widow, Lady Edith (confidante to the governor-general's wife, Helen Munro-Ferguson), federal Parliament voted to return Bridges' body to Australia.

And so, on 3 September 1915, Bridges was buried on a ridge on the north-eastern slope of Mount Pleasant overlooking the Duntroon academy he had created and the floodplain where the descendants of Ainslie's ewes grazed.

In 1916 Griffin – cognisant of the importance of Bean's war memorial and by then designing a memorial for Bridges' grave – tried to resurrect his Capitol by suggesting that it should be the site of the national monument to the war dead *and* Bridges' grave. Taking, as always, the bureaucrats' advice, the politicians rebuked Griffin by pointing out

Parliament had determined Bridges would stay buried overlooking Duntroon.

Griffin understood how war had redefined Australia's disposition. For him the spirit of the Capitol, always intended to embody national sentiment, could easily be enshrined in the war memorial. That's why he felt the memorial should go on Capitol Hill.

While touring Duntroon, I stopped at Bridges' grave on the hill. A conifer stands sentinal at each corner of the memorial, an expanse of white gravel in the middle of which is a simple rectangular polished granite slab. A bronze sword is set into the stone.

Despite all of the thoughts and dreams and years that he dedicated to Canberra, it seems unthinkable that Bridges' grave is the only project that Griffin completed in Canberra.

But it is true.

And so it was that the war memorial went to the other end of the land axis where I now stand, looking opposite to Parliament House.

It find it confounding. One building is revered for its symbolism – the other all too often reviled for its. But how did the reviled come to define my city?

Michael McKernan, historian, writer and former war memorial deputy director, was responsible for finding Australia's 'unknown soldier' and relocating him to the tomb at the base of Mount Ainslie. He says that during his twenty years at the memorial Canberra tourist numbers were determined by visits to his institution.

> There was a guy standing there with a clicker counting because every visitor in Canberra in those days went to the war memorial. The first director of the War Memorial I worked for used to say we didn't get any money from government because our people all came from the western suburbs [of Sydney]. And that is absolutely true. You could see a spike in our numbers every Raiders home game, when the west came down to watch the footy and also stopped in at the memorial. The two best-known institutions in Canberra are the war memorial and the Parliament. Of course everybody loves the war memorial but they hate the Parliament. Why can't they work out that it's the sum of the whole and not just the Parliament?

A few weeks earlier I'd listened to McKernan speak at Tuggeranong homestead about his Canberra experience.

After school, McKernan joined the Society of Jesus. Trainee Jesuits in Melbourne in the early and mid-1960s had fine lives; most studied at the University of Melbourne and they enjoyed active lives – socially and intellectually – within the city's big, influential Catholic community.

Then there was the Victorian Football League competition. Almost as a birth rite, middle-class Catholics from McKernan's school, Xavier College, become members of the Melbourne Cricket Club, entitling them to watch home and away games at the Melbourne Cricket Ground. The young McKernan either watched his team, South Melbourne, or the match of the day at the MCG each week. It was central to his social life.

Then the Jesuits upended his life by sending him to Canberra to study in the General Studies School of the Canberra University College, which had recently been incorporated into the Australian National University. From its inception in 1947 until 1960, the ANU had been a research institution only. The early undergraduates such as McKernan found something of a hillbilly campus

– temporary shed-like structures and a few older buildings – set in paddocks around the Acton Peninsula. It was not the bluestone institution he expected he would attend. Worse, he was accommodated at the Jesuit training institution at Watson, a suburb on Canberra's northern periphery that was bare of trees – and civilisation as he knew it.

'My relationship with Canberra is a love story, but like all good love stories one of the parties wasn't in love at the beginning … I loathed Canberra. No, I hated it,' McKernan explains.

> I should have been at Campion [the Jesuit retreat in Kew, Melbourne] in luxury, I should have been at the University of Melbourne which was a classy university, I should have been mucking around with my Jesuit mates, now that I had more freedom I should have been going to the footy with my Dad every weekend. All those sort of things were taken from me by this ludicrous move up here. I had an uncle who worked for the National Capital Development Commission and was at the NCDC virtually from Day One. He was a strange bloke. He never married. He called the footy, the Australian Rules, for the local radio station 2CA – AFL – you know, Ainslie versus

> Eastlake. Why were they broadcasting football? Because it happened in Melbourne. In those days I reckon probably 70 per cent plus of people were Melbourne exports and like me they all desperately missed the footy.

The absence of a Canberra Australian Rules team in the national competition, the Australian Football League, remains an enduring disappointment to many residents. But the National Rugby League seized the opportunity to harness the city's enthusiasm for a local team in a senior competition in a football code, with the admission in 1982 of the Canberra Raiders. The Raiders have had phenomenal success, building a membership base of about 10 000 from a population of 360 000 and winning three premierships, including consecutively in 1989 and 1990. Besides attracting a big core of traditional NRL supporters, the raiders have garnered support from those whose first game is AFL. (Since 1996, meanwhile, the Brumbies have represented Canberra's proud Rugby Union tradition that dates back to its teams at the military academy, Easts, University, and Norths.)

I don't follow either rugby code – although I am an enthusiastic armchair supporter of the Raiders and Brumbies and I've seen both play at home. Having grown up spending Saturdays (and often Friday nights and Sundays) watching Australian Rules live, with its fiercely tribal club loyalties based on late nineteenth- and early twentieth-century internecine suburban rivalries, one thing has overwhelmed me when I've watched Canberra rugby. When I watch my team Collingwood (my antecedents) play Carlton (they stole the 1915 Grand Final from us), Essendon (Protestant wowsers) or Hawthorn (eastern suburbs toffs), I know why I hate the opposition. But when you support the Brumbies or Raiders you back a team behind which your whole city – not just your suburb – is united. And you can be equally confident the supporters of every other team in the country are gunning for your guys.

David Headon thinks the Raiders' early success had a seminal impact on Canberra's identity and self-esteem.

'Having a team that was so quick to win – in the '87 Grand Final, winning '89, '90 and '94 made a huge difference to the way we saw ourselves. It represented the end of the Victorian connection and the first generation of kids other than the farmers' kids, began embracing the place.'

In his speech at Tuggeranong, McKernan, who

left the Jesuits in his twenties, said Canberra began to mature after self-government in 1989, coinciding with the Raiders' first premiership.

A woman asked: 'Don't you just think that Canberra went to the dogs with self-government – the streets became dirty, the garbage isn't collected properly, and the streets of Civic smell of wee?'

McKernan responds politely that while all this may be true, a city – a real city – has real city social and administrative problems.

I ask McKernan later if Canberra's infamous NIMBY-ness – its obsession with planning matters, especially as they impinge on nature through the 'urban infill', and municipal order – drive him mad, as they do me.

'We are now a mature society and we are a caring community and I think that increasingly we are not much interested in what the rest of Australia thinks about us. But NIMBY and NOTE [Not Over TherE] I mean every time we try and do something someone finds … an earless dragon,' he says, referring to numerous developments that have stalled due to the grassland earless dragon (*Tympanocryptis pinguicolla*), a near-extinct native lizard whose remaining habitat is the capital territory and the New South Wales Southern Highlands.

> We just don't want anything to change and that's the negative side. Yeah, look, I live in a leafy suburb – I'm lucky. We back onto the ridge. Up until fairly recently my wife and I walked up on the ridge every morning. But you suggest we knock those trees over for hazard reduction – God no. Or we should put up a seven-storey block of flats at Kingston on the lake foreshore. God no. So that's the down side.

Most of the native grassland was lost long ago to the graziers. It seems right to me to retain some of what's left so Canberra might at least keep greenbelts between the suburbs that sprawl ever outwards, north, south and west – well beyond the borders of Marion Mahony Griffin's drawings and once isolated settlements that are now estates of bungalows with double garages and basements that demanded their own plazas, schools and medical centres.

And so it is that the Tuggeranong Valley's suburbs have encroached on the old homestead that grew, with renovation upon alteration, around Waniassa, the original stone cottage of Thomas

Macquoid – coffee trader and colonial sheriff who went bust and shot himself through the head in Darlinghurst when returns were low on the Limestone Plains in 1841. In a tragic endnote to the Macquoid story, his son Thomas Hyacinth ('Hya') managed to pay the creditors and return Waniassa to profit before visiting England; returning on the *Dunbar* he and 120 other passengers died when the clipper ship struck Sydney's South Head during a storm in 1857.

A local writer and historian, Jenny Horsfield, shows me around Tuggeranong, as the homestead became when the Cunninghams bought it after the Macquoids died.

Here is the original stone fireplace that Macquoid built, around which now stands the drawing room of the later homestead.

And here is the stone-walled and shingle-roofed barn the convicts built in the 1830s – probably the oldest intact convict-era building in Canberra. I run my fingers over its walls and the grooves, notches and the rope burns in the eucalypt supporting beams. It's a small connection with a convict past in a curious little island of pioneering history standing in the Tuggeranong Valley suburb of Richardson.

Horsfield tells me stories about the Cunninghams – about the hardships of the resilient pioneer Mary, who married a second-generation Cunningham and who was open about her loneliness, isolation and depression; about Mary's son Andy, a daredevil who went off to war in Palestine and returned with a dangerous passion for aeroplanes, which he'd land at nearby Lanyon, and strong drink, which became his undoing; about the tough wanderers who'd blow in for the shearing season; and about the officer cadets from Duntroon in pursuit of the Cunningham girls. The Cunninghams moved from Tuggeranong to Lanyon in 1915. The Commonwealth acquired Tuggeranong in 1917.

The walls of Tuggeranong Homestead are lined with pictures of the past – Andy and his aircraft, the Aboriginal leader Queen Nellie, her husband King Billy, and Charles Bean.

After the war, Bean, in Melbourne, began formatively collating his epic twelve-volume *Official History of Australia in the War of 1914–1918*. But interruptions were constant; diggers kept wanting a piece of him. So he asked the government to find him somewhere quieter. The government came up with Tuggeranong which the Hughes government originally earmarked as the site for an armaments production centre. Bean lived and worked there with a team of researchers and writers from 1919 until 1925.

While there, Bean met his future wife Effie, a Queanbeyan nurse. He rode his horse into the hills and played cricket with his researchers and neighbours. Bean was such a keen cricketer he even laid a concrete pitch in one of the paddocks. I walk through the long grass, mindful of snakes, as Horsfield leads me to the strip of grey cracked concrete standing just a hundred metres or so from one of the busy roads linking the satellites of Tuggeranong.

The war's end and the Great Depression ensured Billy Hughes' armory never eventuated. While the armory was averted, it was a portent of the future face of Canberra where the apparatus and symbols of militarisation would struggle for harmony with the city's democratic ideal.

For many years, Russell Hill has been evolving into an exclusive military precinct. As the journalist Philip Dorling wrote in *The Canberra Times* on

15 August 2009, Russell is 'characterised by the architecture of security and exclusion – high fences, security cameras and crash barriers'. Since 1952 a prominent public monument has towered over the extension of Kings Avenue at Russell, looking down upon the lake and across at the politicians. It is the Australian–American Memorial. Erected in 1952 by the Menzies government after the public subscribed £100 000, as a symbol of Australia's thanks for America's support in the Pacific between 1941 and 1945, the memorial features a stylised version of the American eagle atop a towering plinth.

From the time she could talk, my youngest daughter has referred to the statue as 'the fly'.

Now the southern flank of Constitution Avenue, Griffin's bustling peoples' boulevard, is home to the new ultra-secure $500-million-plus Australian Security Intelligence Organisation building. While this intimidating behemoth of tinted glass, concrete and steel none too subtly plots Australia's security priorities post September 11, it is also a blight on what little remains of Griffin's plan. (Equally illustrative of the encroachment of security into the symbolic heart of Canberra is the new Australian Federal Police headquarters, bordering the Parliamentary Triangle on Kings Avenue.)

Aldo Giurgola, who co-designed Parliament House and oversaw its construction on the original Capitol site, surveys the lake from the expansive windows of his apartment high in a Kingston tower overlooking a postcard vista of Telopea Park, the lake, Mount Ainslie and Black Mountain. The Italian-born ninety-one-year-old has something of a bird's eye view of the developments – immediately below on the Kingston foreshore, at Russell, along Parkes Way, Constitution Avenue and at New Acton – that signify Canberra's recent bureaucratic and higher density residential expansion.

His apartment is open and light. Its walls hold beautiful art and its bookshelves (with titles, among many, on Boccioni, Picasso, Rodin, Venetian villas, Renaissance architecture, the Unicorn Tapestries, Schubert, Beethoven, Haydn) betray a refined aesthetic sensibility.

He is critical of most recent high-density development as architecturally shortsighted and inconsistent with both the topography and the plan of Canberra. While he is a Griffin admirer (as an architecture student in Rome he encountered, almost daily, one of the Griffin drawings of Canberra), he believes too little credit is afforded the early planners and surveyors like Scrivener, who had the foresight to choose this 'remarkable' site.

'I complain about the ASIO building,' he says, pointing through his windows at its long black form on the other side of the lake, 'because it has become like a big retaining wall of dark glass on the landscape … making everything secret … separating the natural slope beneath the mountain [Mount Ainslie] and Constitution Avenue from the lake.'

Giurgola, who took Australian citizenship and moved permanently to Australia after he completed Parliament House in 1988, says Canberra is 'delightful' because it has been 'structured with trees and no other city in the world has this sort of generosity of space'.

He says that during his career 'I always found myself living in places where I found that my work had been appreciated'.

'I have lived in New York. It's a fantastic city.' But it is a city for the young, he says. In Canberra, he says, it is easier to find 'measure' between lifestyle, natural beauty and human ambition.

He gestures to Telopea Park, its treetops bursting with the colours of rust and ripe wheat and blood orange.

'And what more do you need? Down there are trees of every variety and colour.' He smiles.

The ASIO building was always going to go ahead. But meanwhile the influential Memorial(s) Development Committee has lost a fight to place two twenty-metre-high memorials to the two world wars on the northern shores of the lake near the prized land axis.

Does Canberra really need memorials to the two world wars? Apparently. The Australian War Memorial, while intended as a memorial to the 'Great War', had its charter changed to commemorate the nation's dead from all wars.

The backlash against the proposal on cultural and planning grounds, as prominent Canberra residents opposed the memorials, was swift, articulate and highly effective. The local chapter of the Walter Burley Griffin Society, established nationally in 1998 to promote and preserve the Griffins' work, played a prominent role in stopping the monuments from going by the lake.

Brett Odgers heads the Canberra chapter of the Griffin Society. I visit him at his house in Swinger Hill (seriously! Louis Swinger was an important early Canberra surveyor), an enclave consisting mostly of well-lit, architecturally sound and seamlessly integrated low-rise, medium-density dwellings in the inner south. Griffin may well have approved of Swinger Hill – unlike much of the rest of suburban Canberra.

Odgers estimates that at best one-third of the original Griffin plan has actually been achieved in Canberra and that given the eighty or so amendments that have already been approved since 1925, the legacy is continually eroding.

> It's why we fought hard against those [war] memorials. One of the few things that remains of the Griffin plan is that great vista [the land axis]. Griffin ultimately in 1929 endorsed the location of the war memorial there, but he of all people would have admired the fact that the authorities have kept from the war memorial to Capital Hill that unbroken, clear land axis.

When I first read the stories about the 'great battle' over the war memorials, I scoffed at what I saw as the NIMBY-ness of it. It was just the sort of introspected self-obsession I have always felt gives this city a bad name.

But that was when I just lived here. Now I understand the unique purpose of my city. I appreciate that the function of the great triangle – not least its parliamentary zone south of the lake, with its balance of the legislative, the judicial, the cultural and the archival – is to visibly represent Australian democracy in the very landscape. Surely that is worth preserving and enhancing – if not explaining to the Canberra haters? The unbroken line from the top of the legislature at Capital Hill to the Tomb of the Unknown Soldier at the country's most revered secular shrine is critical to that symbolism as it evolved.

Robert Menzies proved that it's possible for someone to change their mind about Canberra.

Menzies, who entered federal Parliament in 1934, considered travelling to and from Canberra a monotonous chore. The only advantage was that all Melbourne-based politicians were subject to the same plight; they got to know each other socially as a result.

The general view of Canberra among the politicians was that of a 'cemetery with lights' – a waste of a good sheep station. But they were in it together in a way that engendered a collegiate atmosphere that is absent from political life today. And they would all be out of Canberra as quickly as possible once the House of Representatives and the Senate rose at the end of each week … except those from the further provinces – Tasmania, South Australia, Western Australia and northern Queensland – who had little option but to spend the weekends here too.

But during his second term as prime minister, from 1949 until 1966, Menzies began to change his mind. He set about changing Australia's mind, too.

In 1955 – the year he established the National Capital Development Commission, to push ahead with the continued development of the city – a Senate select committee report, *Development of Canberra,* quoted him saying:

> I cannot honestly say that I liked Canberra very much; it was to me a place of exile, but I soon began to realize that the decision had been taken, that Canberra was and would continue to be the capital of the nation, and that it was therefore imperative to make it a worthy capital; something that the Australian people would come to admire and respect; something that would be a focal point for national pride and sentiment. Once I had converted myself to this faith, I became an apostle.

The city experienced by Eilean Giblin and her husband Lyndhurst had changed little since war's end. Many major departments still had not entirely relocated from Melbourne. The city itself had hardly grown since the late 1930s. Dusty unmade roads were common. There was still no lake.

In *Cold Light* Campbell Berry, an energetic Lake proponent, gets Menzies – himself a convert to establishing the water feature – to commit £3 million to the project. Menzies then goes overseas. On returning, Menzies convenes a meeting in his Parliament House office with Berry and his Treasurer, Harold Holt, a man, writes Moorhouse, 'who had no smile, only a salesman's grin'.

Menzies asks Berry if she 'got wind of the elimination of the lake money from the budget while I was away?'

Berry says no.

Menzies demands if Treasury struck out the money for the lake in his absence.

Holt replies: 'Cabinet agreed, Ming. Done and dusted. No lake.'

In his 1970 autobiography, *The Measure of the Years,* Menzies wrote:

> … I turned to the Treasurer, who was my good friend and ultimate successor, the late Harold Holt, and said, with what I hoped was a disarming smile, 'Am I rightly informed that when I was away the Treasury struck out this item of one million for the initial work on the lake?' the reply was yes, and that Cabinet had agreed. I then said, 'Well, can I take it that by unanimous consent of ministers the item is now struck in?'

Menzies and his wife Dame Pattie made The Lodge home (his Liberal disciple, John Howard, later refused to make it his). Deakin, Forrest and Manuka were their neighbourhoods. Both were keen walkers. But in his second term, Menzies walked less because people kept stopping in their cars to offer him a lift.

Once Menzies had steamrolled Treasury to get the money, work on the lake began quickly, in line with a vow from the NCDC that it would be finished inside four years. Menzies shrugged off criticisms and dismissed the 'moaners' who insisted that the money could be better spent, while an army of 500 workers cleared trees, houses and other buildings across the Molonglo Valley. By early 1964 (inside the four-year deadline), after decades of argument about its shape and capacity, the excavations for the ornamental waters – with their 6.6 square kilometre surface, forty-kilometre shoreline and 33 million cubic metre capacity – were complete. At last Canberra had the hole for its lake – all it needed was the rain.

Then Menzies gave the city some footpaths, although some suburbs, including mine, still don't have many. I want to get to the bottom of what I'm sure is an apocryphal story that Menzies became further energised about the need to develop Canberra when his wife complained about having to push the prams of her grandchildren along grass and unmade roads.

Regardless of who actually 'gave' Canberra the footpaths, someone had to build them in the 50s and 60s. Venetian-born Manlio Pancino, who came to Australia in 1954, was one who did.

'Coming into Canberra … we looked out the window and thought there must be some mistake – the station was so small … we were divided into groups and taken by truck to different city locations to work laying footpaths which wasn't easy – dirty and dusty. This was our daily routine,' Manlio recalled in his unpublished memoir.

'Capital Hill Hostel had very poor cooking

facilities and there were huge blowflies from the surrounding grazing lands, so maggots in the stew were common.' He took Australian citizenship at the Albert Hall and lived in Canberra for fifty-five years. Manlio, a draughtsman, eventually secured a job at the ANU which he held until his retirement.

I go to see Heather Henderson, the daughter of Robert and Pattie Menzies. She and her husband Peter, a former diplomat, still live in Canberra. Like the homes of so many senior public service families, theirs is filled with artefacts from their travels. There is a bust of Sir Robert in the hallway and some pieces of art once owned by him on the walls.

Heather recounts how she returned from Jakarta, where her husband was posted, to have her first child. She lived in The Lodge with her parents while pregnant, and afterwards, with the baby.

> And then when the baby was born of course my mother was in on the act and she said, 'Bob, you take the baby for a walk. The footpaths are appalling.' And so all this complaining went on and on. And so eventually he said, 'Well, I can see we're stuck with Canberra whether we like it or not. So we might as well do it properly.' And from then on, everything started to move.

There was no need for security at The Lodge, she says.

Eventually someone decided in their great wisdom that there should be a guard at the gate. So they got a guard at the gate – utterly useless. The guard got a bit cold in winter so he would put the radiator on and shut the doors of his little guardhouse. And then they got a dog. And he would walk around with a dog occasionally. My mother always claimed that our little dog was a better watch dog than the big one at the gate.

Mother liked carving. And so when people came for dinner she would carve the roast. And one night she was standing at the sideboard carving and Violet, the parlour maid, came in and said 'Madam' – she was very nervy, poor old Violet – 'there's a man in the kitchen'. So my mother who was very small, still clutching the carving knife, walked out to the kitchen, and the man took one look at this fierce little woman with this carving knife and shot out the back door. And my mother went over to the back door, which was wire at the top and wood at the bottom, and had a little snib. And she snibbed it and she said, 'I've told you before to keep this door locked.' So that was the security at The Lodge. None.

Then I tell Menzies' daughter a small story about my mother.

In 1951, at twenty-five and having worked in the family business, having worked on her big brother's political campaign, and having briefly considered becoming a nun, Mum went to Europe with a couple of her girlfriends. It was an adventurous thing to do back then, before jet travel and while much of Europe was still physically and economically reeling from the war.

She travelled 'the continent' and came back to London where she worked for British Labour at party headquarters at Millbank. She was there during the 1951 general election. Having worked on the 1949 Labor campaign in Australia, she was left unimpressed by the British effort. She said that the workers were lazy, badly organised and lackadaisical – astute observations as it turned out because Prime Minister Clement Attlee's Labour was trounced.

London was still suffering from the effects of the Blitz. The city was depressed and dingy. Fuel and food rationing made life difficult. But Mum had a wonderful time despite all that.

She received invitations to garden parties at Buckingham Palace and, from the moment she arrived, found her name on the guest list at Australia House and at the other Australian diplomatic missions around Europe. We have learnt, since her recent death, that she fell in love with an Irishman while in London. She was considering marrying him. But she came home early when her mother, who was ill, beckoned. It was cut all too short.

She used to endlessly tell stories about the magical times in London to my elder sister and me when we were children. Today, I can see how in middle age, when my mother's frustration with her life was becoming apparent, she conflated events from her time in Europe so that they became something of a nostalgic fairytale. Notwithstanding the joys of her later marriage to my father, and having children, they were I'm sure the very best of days for her.

Mum's connection with Canberra started before her European adventure. It was a rich part of her earlier life before Dad and before us – a life that revolved around her brother, Bill Bourke, the federal member for the Victorian seat of Fawkner, from 1949 to 1955.

My mother's father – also Bill – died when she was seven. William Meskill – Bill Junior

– became his surrogate. She campaigned, along with her older siblings, to help him win Fawkner. She worked in his electoral office and sometimes accompanied him to Canberra. When the Labor Party split, she stuck with her brother, who was aligned with the conservative Catholic Industrial Groups – 'the groupers' – that were in a pitched ideological battle, heightened by the Petrov hysteria, with the party's Evatt-backed Left. When the Labor Party expelled Bill in 1955 and he helped form the Democratic Labor Party she, too, quit the ALP. He lost his seat in 1955.

During his time in Parliament, especially before the bitterness of the espionage royal commission and The Split, Bill had been friendly with Menzies. Their seats in Melbourne adjoined and their political ideologies were not poles apart. Politics was certainly fiercely adversarial. But it was not as angrily partisan as it is now, and leaders generally afforded each other more respect (Menzies was a pallbearer at the funeral of both Chifley – who died at the Kurrajong Hotel in Barton in 1951 where he'd lived even as prime minister – and Evatt, who died in 1965).

I tell Heather Henderson that I had always wondered how Mum had become such a social success in London and how, while going through her papers and her letters after her death, I think I found the answer.

It is a thick piece of cardboard, embossed with the Australian coat of arms and dated 16 March 1951, Canberra ACT.

It introduces my mother, describing her as a 'respected citizen of Melbourne' and asks that she be shown 'any facilities or courtesies which may be accorded' during her absence from Australia.

I tell Henderson that the letter bears her father's signature.

She laughs but does not seem surprised.

> You see, that's an example I think of how politics in the Old House was played quite differently. It was much smaller – they were all in it together. They were opponents, but there were also many close friendships that existed between Liberal and Labor and Country Party that just wouldn't happen today. Today in Parliament they don't debate – it's just screaming at each other. And the place [Parliament House] is just so big that they don't talk outside the chamber.

I leave the Hendersons and drive back to Old Parliament House, where I intend to do more research on the workers who built the place.

But instead I sit on the steps and think about my mother and father and read the Menzies letter again.

When Labor expelled Bill, Mum quit and joined the DLP. She campaigned for the party at successive federal elections. She readily co-opted me as a boy into letterboxing the DLP's anti-Labor, anti-Communist election pamphlets.

Mum and Dad fought about that bitterly. Dad refused to have the DLP flyers in the house. Mum had to secrete them in her car.

And so when we visited Canberra on the family holiday in 1970, for DLP stalwarts like Mum, Whitlam was the *bête noir,* the Black Prince promising to return Labor to power for the first time since 1949.

Mum hated him.

Dad adored him.

My parents had married just after The Split in the knowledge, no doubt, that each viewed it differently. They must have believed in love's all-conquering powers. But by the time I was five or six the pre-existing tensions in their marriage were manifest in their stark political differences. In my family, politics was everything.

The election of Whitlam in 1972 and his dismissal in 1975 were major marital events.

My Grade Six class at the junior school of the Catholic boys' college I attended in Melbourne was interrupted on 11 November 1975 so we could be told the Queen's man had sacked Whitlam. When I arrived home that afternoon, Mum was toasting Whitlam's dismissal with crème de menthe. Later, Dad cursed at the television and the image of Kerr's secretary, David Smith, in his frilly shirt, reading the proclamation dissolving both houses of Parliament while standing on the steps on which I'm now sitting.

I think back to my parents' argument that began here forty years ago when Dad was fawning over Whitlam, the fight that set me against politics and this city from such an early age.

And I recall once again my customarily even-tempered father raising his voice at Mum in the car.

I had forgotten until a few years ago what Dad said to her. But I rediscovered it when, in feeble old age a few years before their deaths they visited me in Canberra still – miraculously I often thought – together, but still in equal measure apart.

In the car that day he angrily said the same thing to my mother that he would repeat to her two years later during the 1972 election campaign, when she had enlisted me, then eight, on one of those many DLP letterbox drops. It was the same thing I heard him say to her, in a quieter tone, when I took them back to Parliament House for lunch during their final visit to Canberra together.

'He was a damn Grouper. A twister and a bloody wrecker.'

For Mum politics was heartbreak. Old Parliament House never fails to remind me of that.

But for others it evokes far more poignant, painful memories.

On 6 March 1941 Eilean Giblin wrote:

> There is a shop arcade at Manuka and at one end of it there is a small open space called The Lawns. Presumably grass once grew all over it, but now there is not much, except in the centre, but there

> are well-grown plane trees and seats here; young women in bright dresses sit in the dappled light and shade or old men reading papers.
>
> There are shops on either side of the open space, and I always think it the most picturesque spot in Canberra, with people coming and going, children on bicycles, and men standing in groups talking ... Canberra is a great place for women with babies in prams ... Attractive they look in their summer clothes with bare legs.

The shops around the open space Giblin describes – which today intersects Canberra's prime boutique strip – have changed. But the plane trees are still there, casting a dappled light onto patchy lawn where the children still play. Now the little square is surrounded by a series of cafés and restaurants, shops selling fine frocks and shoes and expensive holidays. It is the prime location for Canberra's lunching ladies, who dine al fresco in summer on crab linguini, focaccia and salade niçoise, in their colourful dresses and with bare legs.

It is where I catch up with Lyn Mills. Besides being Canberra's first real 'show-biz' reporter for the city's earliest commercial television station, Channel 7 (in the days when ads for sheep dip and stock fencing were standard), and the society columnist for *The Canberra Times* today, Mills is the daughter of one-time Canberra press gallery veteran Ray Maley.

'Dad was Menzies' press secretary when he dropped dead of a heart attack in King's Hall at the Old Parliament House in 1964. He died just before Princess Marina (the Duchess of Kent) arrived at the hall. He was in the receiving line. So the ghosts for me in Canberra are all in King's Hall,' she says.

Elite Canberra society, which Mills writes about and photographs, is small and revolves around the upper echelons of the public service, the business community and the diplomatic corps. Everybody, she says, knows everybody's business: we talk about the addiction of a well-known Canberra identity, about how another has defaulted on loans with creditors and how the wife of a prominent resident has just run off with an alleged criminal. A child of one of the people we talk about walks past.

'I know who's related to who. I know where the bodies are buried,' says Mills. She winks. We order coffee and gossip on.

She reminds me that old inner Canberra, from Turner to Red Hill, is small.

I know. It's always irked me. If ever we needed emergency provisions from the supermarket on a Sunday evening my wife and I, when we were both journalists, would argue about who should go because whichever of us did would invariably encounter somebody we'd written about that weekend.

In the mid-1960s Donald Horne wrote in *The Lucky Country* that 'some of the snobberies of Canberra can acquire a fascination – the Canberra Club life, the smaller diplomatic parties. Officials may see themselves as important national figures when in truth hardly anyone in Australia has heard of them'.

In inner Canberra the dinner parties and restaurant gossip might focus on the clashes between department secretaries and ministers, an indiscreet lobbyist, some press gallery starlet or an infantile *West Wing* wannabe from the prime minister's office. But anywhere else, they're nobodies.

Regardless, in Canberra considerable social cachet is still attached to the departments in a hierarchy beginning with Treasury, the Department of Foreign Affairs and Trade (DFAT), Defence, Finance, and so on, down.

Says Mills:

> Once upon a time not so very long ago there were a whole lot towards the top of the public service who had pretentions. But these days it's much more down to earth. There are still the famous DFAT wives of course – they're famous for living their lives through their husbands. Fancy it, all these people who live in brick veneers in Pearce or whatever, with such delusions of grandeur.

The diplomatic and senior public service cocktail party circuit was famous, until well into the 1980s, for its vacuousness, internecine jealousies – and affairs.

But today, Mills says, ambitious fundraising is the focus of most social activity.

> People are really generous – they donate. These days the functions aren't just about people getting their heads in the paper, which is what it was like for decades. Today it is much more about trying to do something that is good for the community. It's not just swanning around at dinners and pissy bloody cocktail parties where nothing really happens, any more – it's about who can raise the most money for what charity.

While the diplomats like a party, Mills points out that nobody knew quite how to *party* like the academics in the 1970s.

Especially those attached to the English and History departments.

'The writers and the academics – the long lunches and the parties of the 70s?' Mills says. 'Well *hello*.'

Let's sing a song of Canberra, the nation's capital;
It's a very pretty city, but it's got no heart at all.

Chorus:
You get those bad Canberra blues,
Get on the booze;
You get those awful Canberra blues.

We drink a lot of beer here, we've got a lot of
friends,
It's like being at a party, but the party never ends.

I came to this fair city, looking 'round for work,
That was twenty years ago today – I'm still a base
grade clerk.

Go east or west in this fair city, of one thing you
 may be sure.
You'll see the same damn faces that you saw the
 day before.

Chorus

From *Canberra Blues* by Bob Brissenden

The academics and writers who gravitated to the Canberra University College (later the Australian National University) had a fine time in the 60s, 70s and 80s.

Situated on J.J. Moore's old station on what, post-lake, became the Acton Peninsula, the university was a geographically and culturally isolated promontory.

Bob Brissenden, an acclaimed poet, novelist and 60s folk singer (legend has it he once played warm-up for Dylan at a Greenwich Village coffee shop), was a lecturer in English at Canberra University College and later sub-dean of the Faculty of Arts at the ANU. As an active writer and lecturer, and as chair of the Literature Board of the Australia Council from 1978 to 1981, Brissenden, together with other teachers in the 1960s – including Alec

(A.D.) Hope and Dorothy Green – oversaw a burst of literary achievement that demanded the attention of the bluestone and ivy English departments elsewhere. Judith Wright was also on campus in the early 1970s as the recipient of a Creative Arts Fellowship. Two other established and awarded poets, David Campbell and Rosemary Dobson (whose husband, Alec Bolton, established the bespoke Brindabella Press in 1972), were also close to the scene. The young writers who studied at ANU – notably Alan Gould, Mark O'Connor, Kevin Hart, Geoff Page and Philip Mead – received rich encouragement from the veterans. Others who became part, through intent or circumstance, of what in the late 1970s became a vibrant – and competitive – Canberra literary scene include Roger McDonald, Sara Dowse, Marion Halligan and Blanche d'Alpuget.

Students of history, meanwhile, were fortunate to encounter the enigmatic Professor Charles Manning Clark. Some alumni recall that something of a cult developed around Manning Clark, the Professor of History – and later Australian History; so much so that some aped his dress style, with moleskin trousers and Akubra hats.

'I always had the view that if Canberra was a

real national capital it should be attracting to the city the best work that was being produced by the best writers in the country,' says Gould, a poet and novelist. 'And so when we got this journal going, *Canberra Poetry* as it was called, and subsequently got a little letter press going, we would solicit material from the likes of Vincent Buckley or Bruce Dawe or people from all around the place and they sent it willingly.'

Gould came to Australia as a teenager in 1966 after his father, a brigadier in the British Army, was posted to Canberra. He was among those on campus who resisted the Vietnam draft, evading the Commonwealth Police and living between a series of 'safe houses' in Sydney and the ACT.

> I had some wonderful fun. We used to turn up on pillion on the back of a motorcycle and attend these demonstrations on campus, and we'd be watching for the Special Branch and as soon as there was a move on you'd jump on your pillion and you'd be off in dramatic circumstances that were probably more dramatic than they needed to be.

Less fun, however, was the week he spent at Goulburn Prison after turning himself in when two co-dodgers were nabbed.

The poets of and about the university called themselves the 'Acton Circuit'. Besides being a statement of identity, the brand served as a defiant 'up yours' to the intellectual snobbery of other institutions. They were parochial and rightly proud of their artistic enclave; they loved the dusty emerging city, the surrounding bush and nearby coast (Campbell lived near Captains Flat; Wright moved to Braidwood; and Brissenden bought a house amid the spotted gums at isolated Depot Beach).

> I'm a back-blocks academic, which may give rise to
> mirth,
> But selection committees know me well from
> Brisbane through to Perth.
> I've often been short-listed for many a famous
> chair
> But somehow or other, I don't know why, I've never
> quite got there.

From *Back Blocks Academic* by Bob Brissenden

And then there was the social life, including the now legendary boozy 'Poets' Lunches' and the raucous dinner parties and bawdy open-house parties – the best of 'the good times' as the late Canberra wine merchant, Jim Murphy, who quenched the poets, famously said on his TV ads. On campus the Staff Club was the social hub.

So important was this institution to the academics that Brissenden dedicated a poem – *The Staff Centre ABC* – to it. Three letters from this poetic alphabet will probably tell the story.

A is for AFTERNOONS, lazy and long,
Filled with white wine and soda and sunshine and
song.
D is for DRINKING – the theme of our verses!
It makes our hearts merry and empties our purses.
G is for GIRLS and for GROG and for
GLASSES:
When you put them together how soon the time
passes!

ABC journalist Michael Brissenden is the son of Robert. His mother Rosemary Brissenden is a noted international relations academic, who pioneered writing about and cooking Asian food in Australia.

He recalls:

My memories of the academic life of the 60s and 70s in Canberra generally revolve around the serious devotion to drinking, partying and politics. Much of the social life of the ANU seemed to focus on the Staff Club. As I kid I can recall many afternoons spent wandering the grounds there as my parents and their friends had a good time. They had tables set out under the pine trees and the bar was run by Jim Murphy.

There was a wine and cheese appreciation group that used to meet there too quite often. I think the wine was the more important part of the equation. Often Friday afternoon drinks would spill on into the evening. Guitars would come out, songs would be sung, poetry would be read and heated political discussions would inevitably follow. The thing about Canberra in those days is just how small and political it was but also there was a surprising mix and interaction of political true believers. I remember being dragged along to parties where arguments would erupt between people like my father and John Stone [Secretary of Treasury] or [right-wing economist and Treasury Deputy Secretary] Des

> Moore – particularly around the time of the dismissal.

Blanche d'Alpuget moved to Canberra in 1973 with her then husband, a public servant. She stayed for fourteen years and wrote three books, including the biography of her future husband, *Robert J. Hawke,* and the novel *Turtle Beach.* She wrote the novel after separating from her first husband and while living on an Australia Council grant.

'I am actually terrifically grateful to Canberra … It was a generous place for writers because you had access to the National Library and the ANU and all those people at the ANU. And there were no distractions as there are in Sydney,' she says.

Rather than live in the inner south of 'Old Canberra' like so many senior public service families, she and her first husband formed a collective with other families to build *Urambi Village* in the Tuggeranong Valley. Consisting of forty-three tri-level houses and twenty-nine townhouses, the village revolved around communal space that was closed to cars. The children lived in each other's houses and, as they grew, played in the paddocks and swam in the nearby Murrumbidgee. The Griffins would have approved.

Initially, she found the public service culture intimidating and supercilious.

> You could be at a dinner party and really have no idea what they were talking about. I used to find that very irritating. It was also very snobbish. There was a very strong social hierarchy relating to the public service departments. People were also judged quite a bit on which suburbs they lived in. There was Red Hill, Forrest and Griffith, of course, and parts of Yarralumla.

Eventually her social life bridged the public service world and the artistic and academic crowd.

She says that in winter particularly, entertainment revolved around the cinema, dinner parties and adultery – 'quite seriously, one of the great forms of diversion'.

'And then there were dinner parties. Dinner parties and adultery. It was always a problem for hostesses, "Now is her husband on with his wife and if so where will we seat them?"'

Canberra has more than doubled in size since d'Alpuget left. It was, she says, a 'small university and public service town – advanced in its thinking, liberated intellectually and elite'.

> There was an awareness that Canberra people were better paid than the rest of the country ... they were well-educated, leisured, well looked after by the taxpayer, the place was full of politicians and in a bubble where the grit and the anguish of the real outer suburbs of the cities was completely remote. And that's true. There just wasn't any dirt.

Marion Halligan shows me a picture of her street taken soon after she and her husband moved in, in 1964. The place is pancake flat, with the exception of Mount Ainslie in the background, and saplings struggle on a dusty, near-empty road in Hackett.

Hackett was a new suburb on Canberra's northern extremity. It seemed, Halligan volunteers, 'like the dullest suburb in the world'.

'But I quite like it now, because it's close to the centre and now, of course, it's got its taverna,' she says.

Canberra's intended city centre, Civic, has 'street life' – shops, restaurants, bars – on its peripheries. But the centre is literally swallowed by a vast imposing space – Garema Place. Canberra has never had the lively, cosmopolitan city centre Griffin planned. Which is why the suburban shopping strips have become host to social and cultural life. The best restaurants, bars, galleries and music venues have gravitated to the smaller local shopping strips that are well away from the malls. Almost accidentally in older suburbs like Griffith, Hackett, O'Connor, Watson, Ainslie, Lyneham and Deakin, the strip shops have become social hubs. In the newer suburbs and town centres of Tuggeranong and Gungahlin, the effect is intentional.

Canberra people still judge each other by where they live, Halligan says.

'There is a choice in Canberra. You can live in new suburbs in luxury or you can live in old suburbs in rather more ambiguous circumstances. There is a good deal of snobbishness about where you live.'

Canberra has been domestically stratified since the earliest days of the workers' camps – and still is to a large degree.

Halligan has been an astute observer of Canberra society and its cultures and subcultures – from the lunching ladies and bookshop browsers of Manuka to the gay and lesbian-centric Lyneham – since the early 1970s.

I tell her about a literary agent who once sternly

advised me against basing fiction in Canberra or, indeed, even putting the city in a title. She's been there.

> I did a book with seven women writers in the late 80s called *Canberra Tales* which seemed a good idea because of the echo of *Canterbury Tales* and the notion of pilgrimage. Penguin published it. It only sold in Canberra. It didn't sell anywhere else. So then they re-did it under another title. I don't know that it sold very much better under that title. But they decided that *Canberra Tales* – people didn't want to read it.

I admire Halligan's fiction. It opens a window so the rest of Australia might see the life that goes on here, and to understand that a clever, multicultural and vibrant society with all the cosmopolitan indicators – festivals, fine restaurants, artistic communities, street art – coexists with the public service and the national cultural institutions.

> A lot of people said to me it's terrific. I like to read about Canberra as a place where people live, they say they are pleased to find out that Canberra is a kind of normal place after all. I'm quite interested

> in the ambiguities of Canberra because people think it's so prosperous, you know full of fat cats and of course it's not at all. In terms of real wealth there's hardly any here … and there are a heck of a lot more really poor people. It's a bad place to be poor because the rest of Australia thinks there's no poor here.

Canberra has the nation's most severe shortage of affordable housing for the underprivileged, despite having more public housing. Because of the stark social divisions in our suburbs between poor public tenants and middle-class owners, we see the problems and experience the crime. Heroin use and dealing is rife in the middle of my suburb. We know about the stabbing murders and about the social worker who was allegedly raped just down the road. We know about the girls having babies with their half-brothers, about the prostitution and about the troubled children. We ring the police when we hear the screams and the cries at night.

It's one of the great anomalies of old Canberra: the vast middle class is always close to the social problems of the poorest.

Jon Stanhope arrived here as a first-year student at ANU in 1969. He became a lawyer, joined the public service and entered politics. He was chief minister for almost a decade until 2011.

In his student days, he says, Canberra was so sleepy that after a night at the pub you'd have to drive to Yass to buy a hamburger. 'People actually did that if they wanted to eat a hamburger after the pubs shut at 10 pm – until there was a terrible road accident.'

Shy by nature, Stanhope was not a natural politician. But he became probably the most reforming leader of any Australian Labor government for forty years.

He built an ACT prison so that residents would not be jailed at Goulburn; introduced a Bill of Rights; welcomed the placement of a memorial to the *Siev X* asylum boat that sunk in Australian waters in 2001 killing 353 people; and legislated to legalise same-sex partnership.

Stanhope also famously publicised draconian federal anti-terrorism legislation that he considered impinged his citizens' rights.

Tabloids from other cities specialised in pillorying Stanhope ('Stanhope-less') for what they regarded as his boutique Left obsessions. But Canberra liked his ideas – so long as he could also collect the garbage on time.

This is a core Labor town, as countless federal Liberal MPs have been reminded when they've dared wander the streets beyond Manuka and Kingston. Most notably in 2010 Tony Abbott and Joe Hockey, media in tow, went to a supermarket in (as we know it 'the People's Republic of') Ainslie to make a point about the cost of a carbon tax. A couple of angry protesters turned up to object.

The next day, Tony Wright, a long-time Canberra resident, wrote of Ainslie in *The Age*:

> Its Immensely Concerned Citizens are likely to defend very nearly to the death any tree that is threatened by the local government with lopping; high fashion extends to sandals with socks; the suburb's heritage-listed cottages boast organic free-range chicken runs in their backyards; and the horrors of climate change dominate earnest discussion over vegetarian dinners.

Which speaks equally of the perilous civil and municipal path Stanhope had to tread in some suburbs.

So, he participated fortnightly in *Chief Minister Talkback,* a segment on local ABC radio where he would take listener calls about anything.

> I used to almost will people to ring up and engage me on things like same-sex marriage or refugees or the Bill of Rights. I would have loved a conversation about the prison, I would have loved to have given expression to my feelings and thoughts about really significant issues of policy. But almost never. That was my frustration with *Chief Minister Talkback* – because it was almost always about bloody potholes and trees and garbage bins and the state of a playground. But they're all legitimate too. The voters are always right.

Canberra people, he says, 'have not just a very high expectation but also a very strong sense of entitlement and very strong feelings about the responsibilities of government to provide almost instant gratification'.

'It's a consequence of our history as a Commonwealth protectorate that it's taken us a while to accept that we really do need to find out own way.'

(Andrew 'Pipes' Fraser, the son of Jim Fraser, member for Canberra from 1951 to 1970, said constituents rang his father '24/7 about issues there were mainly municipal. … But he was in the phone book and he saw that as a big part of the job'.)

During the bushfires of 2003, which destroyed 500 homes and killed four people, Stanhope stripped to his underwear to rescue a pilot whose helicopter had crashed into a dam.

He led Canberra's grieving – and its rebuilding efforts. Even local opponents lauded his performance.

Others from elsewhere bagged him.

'It is too much to hope that the bushfires in Canberra will lead to a rethink of the role of Canberra in our national life, the development policies which have so systematically turned the "Bush Capital" into a fire trap, and the very existence of the Australian Capital Territory in its present form,' P.P. McGuinness wrote in *The Sydney Morning Herald* on 21 January 2003 while Canberra grieved its dead and its burnt homes.

> Clearly, the bushfire disaster has to be sourced in mistaken policy. The creation of Canberra as a supposedly well-planned 'green' city, or rather a collection of suburbs amongst bush and pine plantations, was always misconceived … The best thing that could be done now, after the victims of the fires are helped to rebuild their lives (though the uninsured should have to bear the cost of their own folly), is to abolish the ACT as it exists, pare it right back to essentials, and let most of its citizens lead normal lives within NSW.

We had been living in London for two years when Canberra burnt, uncertain if we would return to the capital, another Australian city, or stay in Europe. We were frantic about our friends, our neighbours and our house. I read the McGuinness piece, published in the newspaper for which I then worked. I cursed his disgusting sentiments and his heartlessness.

I knew then we would probably return to Canberra to bring up our children, close to the coast and the mountains, surrounded by the bush and amid the public monuments that are now part of our everyday lives.

As a two-year-old, our son had almost drowned

in the semi-frozen pond in the Sculpture Gardens at the National Gallery of Australia. His mother dived in and dragged him from the peaceful depths among the reeds and goldfish. Both younger kids learned to ride their bikes on the undulating forecourt of the High Court, in what is our favourite square kilometre or two of this city between the court, the gallery, the Portrait Gallery, the lake, the science centre Questacon, and my de facto office, the National Library. As babies, both children were breastfed in the sun, on the lawns between the gallery and the lake. We sent photographs of them among the monuments and statues to their interstate grandparents. (We parent more independently in Canberra because so few of us semi-itinerants have parents or nannas or grandpas here. Children so often leave Canberra and stay away for good after school that grandparents have to make do with school holiday visits.)

As toddlers, they marvelled at their elongated coffee-pot faces in the reflection of the polished stainless-steel surfaces of Bert Flugelman's *Cones*, and we still play chasey among the Rodins and Moores.

To live here is to coexist with the national treasures and the monuments.

They are as much a part of our landscape as Red

Hill, where we walked and bird watched and picnicked while the kids were still in utero, and from where we watched our city grow and counted the years passing.

And now the National Arboretum – a dream of Griffin's whereby endangered plants and trees are being cultivated for conservation, science and preservation – is growing on a rise above the lake. It defies the bushfires and the critics. Canberra is full of monuments to its past and present. The arboretum symbolises optimism in its future.

I am sitting in the War Memorial Hall of Canberra Grammar School – the *alma mater* of the writer Alan Gould, among many other notable graduates.

I think about Gould and something he said that I found most intriguing.

'There's a barbarous edge to this town.'

He's right.

This history of this school, this pillar of Canberra society that Gould loved, is worn on the inside walls of this hall, displayed on the wooden honour boards of embossed black and gold.

I look at the duxes.

1961 DH Eastman

In 1995 Eastman, a brilliant but deeply troubled former Treasury officer, was convicted of murdering Australian Federal Police assistant commissioner Colin Winchester.

I had recently stood in the street surveying the unremarkable driveway of the benign house where Eastman killed Winchester with two bullets to the back of the head, when the policeman got home after work.

The tree where Eastman hid has been removed.

I watched part of Eastman's trial in 1995. He swore at the judge, threw a glass of water from the witness box and repeatedly sacked his lawyers. He then represented himself and was convicted on strong circumstantial evidence – including firearm residue in the boot of his car.

I thought Eastman was bonkers – and dangerous. I know of many he's threatened.

But there is lingering doubt about whether he's the murderer.

Jack Waterford, editor at large of *The Canberra Times* – the paper where he has worked for his entire forty-year career in journalism – has cast serious doubt on the circumstantial evidence that convicted Eastman.

'I've never been satisfied that he did it … Eastman is mad and he is paranoid and he is schizophrenic and all of those sorts of things. Dangerous up to a point. He certainly speaks very violently,' says Waterford.

'Eastman is the son of a Canberra bureaucrat. He follows the processes of hierarchy. Eastman would never have killed a mere assistant commissioner. Not until he had exhausted the commissioner and probably the governor-general.'

Waterford is a genial giant of a bloke, a traditional journalist who likes to leave the office and talk – and talk. We sit at Portia's, a Kingston restaurant as famous for its duck pancakes as it is for hosting politicians and their staff.

I ask him about the suicide in 2007 of another AFP Assistant Commissioner for the ACT, Audrey Fagan. Fagan killed herself while on leave. She was under enormous pressure, not least from Waterford, over her management of ACT Policing. Two weeks earlier he had written in *The Canberra Times* that the territory had been 'receiving a second-rate service at Rolls-Royce cost' and that ACT Policing 'was a complacent and unaccountable organisation of no great competence which is wide open to and may have already been percolated by corruption'.

Waterford shakes his head

'I wear Fagan heavily on my conscience. Not that I would have done anything differently, but because in my own judgment of myself I actually ought to have realised that she was more fragile and less of what you might call a public personage, than I fancied,' he says.

We talk about what Canberra people are like. He refers me to Allan Hawke's report, *Canberra: A Capital Place*.

It found: Canberra has the largest average house size in the nation, which is already the largest in the developed world; 9.2 hectares is needed to support the energy footprint of each person; 75 per cent of Canberrans live in detached dwellings; there is twice the level of public housing as the national average; Canberra is ten times less densely settled than Sydney or Melbourne; over half the ACT is protected in conservation reserves; electricity and gas consumption is outgrowing the population; and car use exceeds the national average.

Waterford says:

> The net wealth of the average Australian is significantly higher than anywhere else … if Australia has the highest standard of living in the world, then Canberra has the *very* highest in the world because the standard of living in Canberra is significantly higher than anywhere else in Australia … you won't find a whole settled essentially stable community that is so smug, so bourgeois, so comfortable, so well educated. I mean this may be fucking paradise. I'm not saying it is. But it's as good as it gets.

The city's clever population (my neighbours have included a scientist, a successful artist, an underwater warfare chief, a terrorism expert, an economist and a former prime minister) makes it challenging at times for the paper that serves it.

> This place has got a bloody expert on everything in the world. By and large untapped. There are people here who know about ancient Icelandic languages. There are people here who've just got a Nobel Prize in chemistry. At *The Canberra Times* you are banned more or less from saying this is 'the first' or 'the biggest' because without doubt somebody will ring up and correct it. In Canberra

> we do look out to the world … This is the cosmo capital of Australia in the sense that everybody is engaged with the wider world.

In the 70s and 80s, the live music scene was at its zenith. Its big venues, like the ANU Bar, the Cock and Bull at the Civic Hotel, the Griffin Centre, Cafe Jax, the Ainslie Rex and the Workers' Club meant it could lure the best acts from interstate to appear with the home-grown bands. Major overseas acts – The Cure, XTC, Magazine, The Fall and Simple Minds – came.

But the groundbreaking local bands, like Young Docteurs, Guthega Pipeline, Falling Joys, the comedy troupe Doug Anthony All Stars, Club of Rome, Moral Majority and Gadflys (and their many off-shoots and sub-bands), used to draw crowds of four and five hundred. It began with Rock Against Boredom, a regular event pitched at the kids of public servants in the late 1970s.

Says Michael Brissenden:

> The big thing for kids in the 70s was the drug scene. Once punk hit so did the … heroin explosion and so many people got caught up in that. It was – and probably still is to some extent – a very permissive sort of place. There were a lot of kids with high-achieving dysfunctional parents and not many distractions.

Marcus Kelson, the son of a former senior public servant, was among those captivated by Rock Against Boredom. Lured by The Clash to London in 1981, he returned a year later to study, and he eventually started a family. He is the city's foremost music journalist. He and his wife Virginia, a senior public servant, travel frequently and both engage heavily with local cultural events and identities – including Christopher Latham's magnificent Canberra International Music Festival, and the National Folk Festival of 2012 where they played mandolin and violin competently, before a crowd of 200. Neither had played an instrument eight weeks earlier. They live in Gungahlin.

I ask Marcus if Canberra is enough for people like them.

Maybe not. But I have filled our house with art and music. And there's an argument I've always felt that you don't really need to live in any particular place to fill yourself with that sort of stuff. It doesn't matter where you are. We went to New York and I made a beeline for all the art galleries. I lived in London and all I did in that year was spend all my time at the National Gallery and at the Tate and at the British Museum.

We have given our kids too much intellectual succour, I hope ... because I've had the experience of living in those other places and I've brought them back with me. And there's an awful lot of like-minded people in Canberra ... if you can send your kids away with a bit of philosophy, a bit of the understanding of The Bible, a bit of the understanding of film and sense of history and music and art, they can understand life.

I am walking the hills with the dog. She is off the lead and a monster 'roo – so big it is almost a caricature that belongs in a *Crocodile Dundee* movie or something – bounds across our path. The dog chases it. The 'roo bounds maybe fifty metres ahead of us and the dog holds fast, yapping at its ski-like feet.

Suddenly the 'roo stops, turns and stands up. The dog jumps. The 'roo stands its ground. The dog leans forward, the hair on her back rising, and growls. The 'roo moves forward while I try to get the dog back on the chain.

My phone rings. The big kangaroo stares down at us and bounces off.

It's a friend who's rung to say the actor Guy Pearce had bagged Canberra during a TV interview in the US.

The local media were angry. The next day Pearce apologised, saying he'd been a 'dickhead'.

Everyone expected Robyn Archer to buy in – to attack Pearce.

Judiciously, she didn't. South Australian-born Archer has had a long, stellar career as a writer, actor and creative director.

I think Canberra100 will be her toughest job yet.

'Any time anybody says nothing happens in Canberra I say "you're crazy". From my position I see everything that's going on. I'm the receptor of little things that arise from the community, I'm on all of the embassy invitation lists, I'm on the local and national institution invitation lists ... all the sporting events. So I'm just getting the lot,' she says.

> It's an incredibly busy town, but it's hidden to most people – what we are trying to do is a reveal. If the fingers are flat out like that [she places her hands flat] and people think it's flat and nothing's happening, then what we are trying to do with the centenary is go like that – [she turns her hands around wriggling the fingers] it's a wiggler – there are people going all over.

Archer says it is inconceivable that Australian political leaders and sections of the media would so blithely abuse another community of 366 000 people to the point that the residents 'are effectively told they are of no value'.

> My experience is that when you get an opportunity to go to Canberra to do something there is a real sense of occasion. I've been saying more recently that whether that's in anger, in a protest, or whether it's in a more positive [way] there is a real sense of occasion. People feel that

> their ideas are important when they are invited to say them in Canberra, as nowhere else – a sense of pilgrimage. You know other cities are great to be in and they are beautiful and you can do lots of different things and there's lots of things to do and lots of restaurants and all that. But there is a sense of occasion about Canberra. And the nearest you probably got to a national recognition of that was probably the 'Apology' [to the Stolen Generation]. Because it was the right thing to say in the right place with the right audience ... but when else does anybody really feel like that's the moment?

The Apology would have happened in Griffin's Captol, I'm sure – if the Capitol ever lived. Instead it took place in Aldo Giurgola's new Parliament House, the telecast shown on big screens out the front to the thousands milling around O'Malley's foundation stone.

It is late February 2012 when I make my first visit to Parliament House for the year.

The inevitable showdown between Rudd and

Julia Gillard is happening. Such moments are always intensely exciting around Parliament. I go briefly to the corridor outside the caucus room where the vote is happening and find it so jammed with media – the blokes pumped and energised, the young TV women dressed as if for the Melbourne Cup – that I vacate quickly.

I'm still captivated by politics. But I no longer have the passion to stand on that frontline.

I return to the building's centre and find a table outside the coffee shop.

The television carries live footage of the crowd down where I've just been. The tables around me are full of lobbyists and staffers waiting for the result.

I sit and watch as ABC journalists interview other ABC journalists in different parts of the building, killing time while Labor tries to extricate itself from its leadership mire.

A man sits next to me at the table. He, too, seems transfixed by the drama that unfolds, as Gillard, predictably, emerges the winner and Labor members vacate the caucus room.

But he has been at the centre of far more momentous dramas.

He is David Smith, the former secretary to Kerr who had read the proclamation in 1975.

And, of course, I am suddenly standing back on the steps of Parliament House forty years ago as my father lifts me up to shake hands with Edward Gough Whitlam.

Epilogue

Twenty years ago as the illegally parked removalists unpacked my possessions, Canberra had just turned eighty.

Nobody talked much about the identity of the place, let alone defended it.

The retired public servant in fawn slacks berating the removalists seemed to be some staged stereotype sent to test my resolve on my first day in the new city.

'It's a public space and besides, the wheels will ruin the lawn.'

I knew what was going to happen next.

'Fuckin' Canberra,' cursed one of the prison-tattooed heavy lifters through missing teeth. 'Full of government pricks what know better on everything. What are you movin' here for, you stupid bastard?' he asked.

Fawn Slacks heard him.

'There's no need for that. I'm happy to point

you to the relevant ACT Government by-law about parking on a nature strip governed by a "No Parking" sign,' he said. 'I should know – I *am* secretary of the body corporate here.'

'Congratulations,' jail tatts returned at my new neighbour. 'And I'm secretary of the Royal fuckin' Australian College of Removalists. And I say the van's stayin' right fuckin' put.'

After unloading, the boys parted with a clutch burnout (no simple feat in a vehicle that size), tearing a strip of lawn from the nature strip.

Hours later the body corporate formally complained in writing – and also about the '*unsightly*' empty cardboard packing boxes stacked on my front balcony '*in plain view of the street*'.

I screwed the letter up, threw it off the balcony. It landed on the recently hosed terracotta tiles on the patio, immediately below, of the body corporate secretary.

Thus began my time as a resident here.

Welcome.

On that first day I vowed I'd give it six months. A year – tops.

I had not owned walking shoes or a bicycle since I was twelve. But I soon owned a pair of Rossi's and a tent, I quit smoking (they were starting to ban it inside, anyway) and began riding my hybrid bike around the lake.

The coffee was bad, although it's better now. The restaurants were good and plentiful, but the service was mostly terrible. That has improved too.

It was true, as my editor had assured me, that Canberra was alive with single, attractive, smart women.

My future wife and I worked in the press gallery together. But we didn't meet properly until – consistent with the young journalists' and political staffers' pattern of long days in the house and late nights of drinking – we met in a bar in Manuka.

She's the reason I stayed, for which I'm thankful. Two of our children were born at the Canberra Hospital in Woden Valley.

One was conceived (in the tent) on the banks of the Cotter.

We bought a house that looks down over the Limestone Plains, but restlessness was never too remote and we were never quite sure how long we'd stay. We moved to London, where I thought we might be forever.

But our Australian-born son became afraid of the outdoors and insects, as we structured his life around the European winter and formal play dates.

We watched the fires on TV in our Fulham terrace while the snow turned to slush on our doorstep. We knew soon after we'd return.

As we flew back into a Canberra parched by drought, our terrified boy looked out the window and down at the dusty yellow plain below, scarred with the charcoal streaks of bushfire damage. The boy had no memory of Australia.

'Mum,' he said, 'you promised we were moving to a real city. There's no city here.'

Yes, we had returned to a Canberra that was still unfinished, as it remains today. But a century after Canberra began, it is, miraculously really, a continuing city.

Lenore wept with happiness.

We were where we should be.

Afterword

It ended as it began almost two-and-a-half decades earlier – in haste with a job offer, this time in Sydney, a city I'd relished visiting but never desired to live in.

I had become a Canberran with solid bona-fides. After living in London for a few years I'd even chosen, despite many warnings I'd find re-entry claustrophobic and stifling, to return to Canberra rather than another bigger city – Melbourne or Sydney – with more urban grit and density.

When the unanticipated change came, I was a Canberra person living in the place where I planned a continuous writing – and personal – life surrounded by the bush that had been my steady emotional and creative muse for so long. I'd never contemplated the prospect of permanently leaving the city to which I felt almost umbilically connected. And I'd finally seen it begin to thrive and blossom, partly consistent with Walter Griffin's original vision, despite all of its historic and ongoing impediments. I had even assumed that one day I'd be interred in the ground thereabouts.

I was content with that idea. Despite hailing from Melbourne, Canberra was where I felt I belonged, the place that harboured me with safety, certainty and all the natural and intellectual beauty that had captivated and inspired me for so long.

You might live in the same house in the same location for twenty years and never find 'home'. Or circumstances – personal, professional, creative, domestic, geographic – may never fortuitously align as they did for me in Canberra. You know when you've found the place where you want to end up. I've always thought that finding a precious connection to place, to a part of the country and its human and other creatures, is to be fully earthed, literally, figuratively. My circuitry felt complete in Canberra.

Home is also where your memories and your spirits dwell. Mine were – and for the time being mostly remain – in Canberra.

I try to view life as time and experience invested rather than 'spent'. And I invested twenty years in that city and the much-loved house, ramshackle and warm, that looked north across the treetops and the Limestone Plains. I wrote six books in that house, including this one, and millions more words besides, and raised children and dogs and nurtured friendships.

Three of our parents died while we lived there. Now it's as if my recollections of them are framed by that house, no longer ours, and planted in that landscape, where they spent so much of their later years with us and their grandchildren and the dogs.

Memories of my parents and my mother-in-law (who could solve any maths homework problem, recite an obtuse Presbyterian hymn, oversee piano practice, do a load of washing and feed the dogs all while carbonising my cooking pots as she made dinner for the kids) are nearly all set in Canberra, about that house and seeded across the city and its bushy heights.

Since leaving I've wondered what happens to our recollections and experiences and words, written and spoken – whether they will always belong to the place where they eventuated. Do the spirits of our dead loved ones continue to dance on the stages where our memories of them were created, and what happens to those spirits when we, the living, move on?

I've never been superstitious. But I just don't sense their presence in my new city. It feels like we've left them behind.

Along with the majestic golden ash into which were carved the initials of our kids, including those of the girl, Evie, who died before birth. And the door-jamb recording the year-to-year heights of the children and every guest (friend, relative, tradie). It was our visitor's book – at once the calendar of years past, and our diary … lost now, painted over with brutal finality just before we locked up.

Despite the glittering, seductive allure of what lay three-and-a-half hours up the Hume, there was a painful wrench in the departure for all of us. It's taken me this long to understand my sadness.

I return often, always with an eye for what's changed.

And each time, I think of the inscription on the pioneering Webb family's gravestone in St John's cemetery: *For here we have no continuing city but seek one to come.*

The city is arrived, just as it continues to

shape-shift with ever-refined architectural and landscaped definition, social and cultural texture.

Stage-one of a light-rail, drawn as a tramway a century ago in those stunning Mahony-Griffin plans, now links Gungahlin to Civic. It happened controversially; the Liberal Opposition condemned it as a waste of money. They claimed costs would likely blow-out as they had with Sydney's light rail, even though all research showed it would become the life-giving infrastructural artery to the vitalisation of the inner-north. It has transformed the heart of the city, and linked the remote outer to the inner in clean, green style. The city is so much better for it. Residents – even many sceptics – have embraced the tram (which came under time and cost).

The light rail section along Northbourne Avenue in the inner-south from Lyneham is lined with newly-vacant lots and demolition sites. The frames of medium-density apartments under construction trace a main northern entry into the city that was until recently imbued with a Soviet ambience and architectural hospitality (thanks to block-after-block of run-down government housing) reminiscent of outer-Minsk or -Vilnius.

The crane is king of the Canberra skyline as

a combination of the urban medium-density residential, hospitality and retail buildings envisaged by the Griffins finally takes shape. The economy booms.

New hotels, their crisp, angular lines of granite, metal and smoked glass, open with optimistic regularity along Northbourne where previously stood the modest housing blocks in red-brick and pale render, their awnings dangling, windows smashed and access stairwells filled with detritus. One street back, nestled amid yet more apartments, is Canberra's hipster Ground Zero: Braddon with its watering holes and eateries, its neon lights and music and people – people who bar-hop and dine at street-side tables and parade as the Griffins dreamed they should, European-style in sweltering, freezing, dusty (smoky) Antipodean Canberra. All in defiance of those fusty Anglophile planners who wanted none of that and nearly wrecked the infant capital with their obstinate wowser-ism!

Another Griffin dream, Constitution Avenue – an anchor of their superb (but largely unrealised) geometric design – is also finding its metier as they envisaged it. They dreamed and drew Constitution Avenue as a bustling peoples' boulevard of apartments and entertainment venues, bars and cafes – a place to see and be seen. Instead it became a barren drag-strip lined with drab 1960s government buildings and the sprawling, architectural indulgence of the above-ground carparks that served them. Now the apartments are going up, with cafes, restaurants and bars on their ground floors.

But there is an onerous social reshaping and cost to some of the new inner-urban development.

As we were preparing to leave the city, the developers were demolishing the vast estate of public housing on our doorstep. Over a decade or so 'the flats' – as everyone referred to them – diminished in their occupancy rates and physical condition. They were badly run-down, fewer families lived there and the estate was beset with social problems and crime (a number of rapes and violent deaths happened in the final years we lived nearby).

For twenty years the word had been out that when redeveloped the flats would be a mix of private and social housing. But like so much of the land of the inner-north and -south – where public housing had been built in the sixties – it was worth a fortune to the residential developers who've always enjoyed significant sway over Canberra's civic decision-makers.

It's all being transformed into prime real estate,

streets of million-dollar-plus dwellings – with not a single unit of social housing. And so, the most valuable, sought after parts of Canberra around the inner-north and -south will be largely devoid of government housing for the poor and less fortunate, most having been re-built on the city's outer-margins. The trade-off for public tenants was old-for-new. But many will find themselves more isolated, further from shops, schools and accessible public transport. As a result, the city's reputation (at least among its own) for social egalitarianism is diminished.

Canberra's poor, already invisible to a nation that tends to view the capital as a vast middle-class enclave of over-entitled public employees, now have a future far less conspicuous, their inner-urban footprint erased from the most desirable parts of the city imposed on the Limestone Plains.

The city continues to grow without them amid its most notable landmarks at either end of the land axis – Parliament House and the Australian War Memorial. Neither were conceived by Walter Griffin nor drawn by Marion Mahony Griffin, taking the southern and northern situations respectively of their conjured Midway Pleasance and Casino, and the peoples' Capitol. Both, nonetheless, it seems, are fixed ever more disproportionately in national psyche and emotional life – each for the wrong reasons.

Australia's latest prime minister, the fifth since this book was first published in 2012, is a former treasurer – just like another PM, Harold Holt. Frank Moorhouse characterised Holt with Exocet accuracy in his novel *Cold Light*, set in Canberra, as a man 'who had no smile, only a salesman's grin'.

This presciently – deliciously – befits the incumbent, an Olympic blusterer and obfuscator, Trumpian in his strategy of dismissing unwanted inquiry with crude distraction. Unwelcome questions – about his government's inaction on climate change and carbon mitigation, ministerial venality and lies issued by his office – exist, without warranting answer, he says, only in 'the Canberra bubble'. By which he seems to mean Parliament House, though his words are deliberately ambiguous to incorporate the whole city. That it demeans the polity, his office, the city, seems of little concern to the grinning salesman.

His is the type of primitive messaging about the capital's supposed detachment from Australian everyday life that's been levelled for political advantage at Canberra as a national capital and as a designed city since the first parliament opened on the plains in 1927. Yet the city continues, thriving and inured to it, after almost a century of similar, hackneyed pejoratives.

Australia burnt. Australia wept. The nation watched appalled and sympathetic as the fires burnt the south coast and crept closer to Canberra, while acrid smoke engulfed the city like it was trapped in some actual giant atmospheric dome – a real bubble. And Australians fixated in anger at the indolence of the sloganeering prime minister, choking inside his bespoke bubble of self-satisfaction. The smoke remains in his eyes, the soot on his collar, as Australia warily suspends judgment over his government's response – coordinated from the city he so readily derides – to the public health and economic threat of coronaviris.

Meanwhile at the other end of Griffin's axis another salesman, this one of gauche sentimentality, invited arms manufacturers into the war memorial to sponsor the telling of the story it enshrines. The merchants of death coughed-up their spare change to have their sponsorship plaques affixed to the walls of our secular shrine honouring those their weapons killed, closing the circle on the military-industrial-commemorative complex. Arms manufacturers – their giant billboards eulogising the weapons of war now also providing the welcome at Canberra Airport – further inflate the story of Anzac, as spun by the memorial's last director, at the expense of so much other history and national memory. Not least the frontier wars that killed tens of thousands of Indigenous people. What would those peacenik Griffins make of it? Something else about Canberra to further break their hearts …

Just as well continental memory, one of the bedrocks of Canberra's national purpose, is so discerning. All sorts of hucksterism – mawkish, fearmongering, cheap, profligate, sentimental – makes its way across Canberra's stage. But it says something about the system to which Canberra is dedicated that the hucksters rarely win in the long run. They are subsumed into the bigger narrative.

That's because the Australian narrative that Canberra serves reaches back sixty-thousand – perhaps even a hundred-thousand-plus – years. The continent has a long memory. The place that serves it best continues to do so, for all its beauty and pain.

When I finally understood that, the city made

sense to me. The pieces fell into place and I live with that knowledge every day. I miss it now. But my experiences – my memories and my spirits – are still there in the ever-continuing city.

Notes and Acknowledgments

The Plains

Anne Jackson-Nakano's book *The Kamberri: A History of Aboriginal Families in the ACT and Surrounds* (Aboriginal History Monograph 8, 2001) is considered to be among the most authoritative published works on the history of the Ngambri people and the emergence of the Ngunnawal. It has deeply informed my writing about the Ngambri before white settlement and about the different tribes that inhabited the area around what is today's Australian Capital Territory.

So, too, have my many invaluable personal discussions, email exchanges and telephone conversations with Shane Mortimer, an elder of the Ngambri (Kamberri) people and a direct descendant of Ija Ngambri and James Ainslie. Shane advised me on the lineage of different prominent Indigenous people of the region, including the Deumonga brothers, Nellie Hamilton and 'King Billy'. Together Shane and Paul Hodgkinson – an agronomist and native grassland specialist – helped me to describe the plains before white man, cattle and rabbits, for which

I am grateful. I am also appreciative of the advice of Margo Neale, a senior curator at the National Museum of Australia and Principal Indigenous Advisor to the director, about the Ngambri people and the varying language groups, including Ngunnawal.

The quotes attributed to John Gale about Canberra's pioneering history come from his 1927 book *Canberra: History and Legends Relating to the Federal Capital Territory of the Commonwealth of Australia* (A.M. Fallick & Sons, Queanbeyan, 1927).

My account of the Throsby/Wild and Throsby-Smith explorations beyond Lake George to the Limestone Plains are based largely on the *Official Year Book of the Commonwealth of Australia, 1931* (ABS cat. no. 1301.0); *A Brief History of Canberra* by Frederick Watson (Federal Capital Press, Canberra, 1927); and R.H. Cambage's 'Exploration between the Wingecarribee, Shoalhaven, Macquarie and Murrumbidgee Rivers' in the *Royal Australian History Society Journal*, Vol. VII, 1921. The account of the further explorations of Wild, Currie and Ovens was drawn from *Canberra's First Hundred Years* by Frederick Walter Robinson (W.C. Penfold and Co., Sydney, 1924) and a speech by Henry Selkirk, 'The Origins of Canberra', a paper delivered to the Royal Australian Historical Society on 29 August 1922 (especially p. 4), which I read at the National Library of Australia's Petherick Reading Room.

The story about Ija Ngambri leading James Ainslie to the Limestone Plains with his sheep has been cursorily – and for the most part inaccurately – covered by the early Canberra histories. I have used a version of the story that has been handed down through the Ngambri generations to Mortimer, who then shared it with me. The Ija Ngambri/ Ainslie story was told with far greater accuracy in the *Canberra Historical Journal* (Canberra and District Historical Society) of September 1978 (p. 20). The early Canberra histories, meanwhile, diverge significantly on the number of sheep Ainslie had with him; Mortimer and Hodgkinson provided me with a copy of the receipt, signed by Ainslie, stipulating the number of stock was 710.

I based the story about Napoleon's willows on what appears to be a first-hand account by Gale that was later repeated in *The Canberra Times* of 17 February 1940.

Frederick Slater's assertion that Ija Ngambri's answer to Ainslie about where they were, meant 'I'll tell you by and by', was published in *The Sydney Morning Herald* on 31 January 1934.

I am indebted to Rowan Henderson, the curator of social history at the Canberra Museum and Gallery, for kindly sharing her hitherto unpublished extensive research on James Ainslie with me. Ainslie is one of Canberra's most significant and mythologised historical figures. As the city's centenary nears, Canberra will have to acknowledge, perhaps, that he was not all he – and many others – said he was.

The reference to J.J. Moore's letter about 'Canberray' comes from Robinson (p. 2) and Moore's 1831 correspondence regarding 'Canburry Creek' from Selkirk (p. 11).

Throughout the book, but especially in 'The Plains' chapter, my writing about the genesis of 'Canberra' was informed by *Aboriginal Place Names: Naming and Re-naming the Australian Landscape* (ANU EPress and Aboriginal History Incorporated, Canberra, 2009), not least in relation to St John's being the first to claim the name (p. 156).

Allan Hawke has been as great a supporter of this project as he is of Canberra. I based my stories about his antecedents Joe Blundell, Isaac Beaumont, their wives and children on his extensive research. I thank him for sharing his – and their – important Canberra stories, and also for his advice on other aspects of my research including the city's complicated leasehold arrangements.

Thanks, too, to Arnold Thomas, for sharing his family story about the tragedy of Mary Ann Brownlow (Guise).

The stories about early Gungahlin and the Palmer and Davis families were drawn from Gale and *A Short History of Gungahlin* (Canberra Archaeological Society, Canberra, 2010), by Helen Cooke.

Nellie Hamilton's 'I no tink much of your law' speech is variously recounted in the early Canberra histories. I drew my version of it from the handwritten memoir of pioneer Samuel Schumack (NLA, MS 1643) held by the National Library. All other references to Schumack are drawn from this document.

The account of John Lhotsky's journey and observations is from *A Journey from Sydney to the Australian Alps, Undertaken in the Months of January, February, and March, 1834: Being an Account of the Geographical & Natural Relation of the Country Traversed, its Aborigines, &c.* (NLA, MS 6350). The bushranging stories are based on the writings of Gale, Schumack and Frederick Watson, as well as William Davis

Wright's *Canberra* (Andrew, Sydney, 1923). The account of OnYong's death and burial comes from Davis Wright.

My description of Duntroon today is based on my guided visit in late March 2012. I thank the Australian Defence Force for arranging the tour – and my guide on the day, Lieutenant Colonel Ian McLean.

G.G. Perceval's colourful recollections of Duntroon and Queanbeyan I found in the boxes of correspondence of the early newspaper proprietor, A.K. Murray, held by the National Library (NLA, MS 3538/Folder 3). The observations of a 'visitor in 1872' form part of the permanent *National Capital* exhibition at Canberra's Regatta Point.

The comments of the MP David McGrath were reported in *The Canberra Times* on 26 July 1928.

Monuments in the Grass

Eilean Giblin's 'War Diary', held by the National Library of Australia as part of the collected papers of her husband Lyndhurt Falkiner Giblin (NLA, MS 366/6/1), are an invaluable record of life in Canberra in the late 1930s and early 40s. All further mention of Eilean Giblin's writing refers to this diary.

Paul Reid's book *Canberra Following Griffin: A Design History of Australia's National Capital* (NAA Publications, Canberra, 2002) informed my writing about the Griffin design and the clashes between Walter and the bureaucrats. Extracts are included with the permission of the National Archives of Australia.

Distinguished Canberra historian David Headon's *The Symbolic Role of the National Capital* (Commonwealth of Australia, Canberra, 2003) and another book to which his research was instrumental – *The Griffin Legacy* (National Capital Authority, Canberra, 2004) – have been critical to my understanding of the design and building phases of Canberra. So, too, have his booklets *Canberra: Those Other Americans* and *Canberra: Crystal Palace to Golden Trowels* (ACT Government, Canberra, 2009). The latter publication was critical to my understanding of the influence of the colonial exhibitions on the aspirations for federation and the capital. David, who is quoted intermittently throughout the book based on our face-to-face interviews, phone conversations and email exchanges conducted in 2011 and 2012, has generously supported me throughout this project. Thanks David.

Greg Wood's booklet *Canberra: The Community that Was* (ACT Government, Canberra, 2009) is among several sources about the plague rabbits. Alexander Oliver's account of his visits to some of the would-be capital sites is published in *A Short Review of the Contents of the Report of the Commonwealth Commissioners on Sites for the Seat of Government of the Commonwealth* (NSW Legislative Assembly paper no. 177 of 1903).

Roger Pegrum's *The Bush Capital: How Australia Chose Canberra as its Federal City* (Hale & Iremonger, Sydney, 1983) was an invaluable source of background material regarding the 'battle of the sites', and the laconic observation about Oliver being an 'outdoors man with a love of the sea …' comes from p. 54 of his book. Alexander Oliver was quoted, also with permission, from *The Bush Capital*, pp. 49–50.

Alasdair McGregor's *Grand Obsessions: The Life and Work of Walter Burley Griffin and Marion Mahony Griffin* (Lantern, Melbourne, 2009) is rightly regarded as the ultimate biography of this remarkable couple. Together with Christopher Vernon's *A Vision Splendid: How the Griffins Imagined Australia's Capital* (National Archives of Australia, Canberra, 2002) and Mahony Griffin's *The Magic of America* (www.artic.edu/magicofamerica © 2007, The Art Institute of Chicago), it was a critical primary source of biographical material on both figures, and of insights into their Canberra experience.

Mahony Griffin's quotes from *The Magic of America* are reproduced with the permission of Ryerson and Burnham Archives, The Art Institute of Chicago.

My biographical material on King O'Malley came from three primary sources: A.R. Hoyle's *The American Bounder* (Macmillan, South Melbourne, 1981), Larry Noye's *O'Malley MHR* (Neptune Press, Geelong, 1985) and exhibits from the 2011–12 exhibition, *King O'Malley*, at the Canberra Museum and Gallery. Charles Studdy Daley (no relation) confirmed in his posthumously published memoir *As I Recall: Reminiscences of Early Canberra* (Mulini Press, Canberra, 1994) that he considered O'Malley an imposter and unworthy of having a suburb named after him.

Gale's eloquent and convincing speech to Queanbeyan, *Dalgety or Canberra: Which?* was later published by Hale & Knox, Queanbeyan, 1907, and distributed widely. I read it at the National Library of Australia.

Hugh Mahon's instructions to Scrivener regarding the site of Canberra is in *Information, Conditions and Particulars for Guidance in the Preparation of Competitive Designs for the Federal Capital City of the Commonwealth of Australia* (Department of Home Affairs, Melbourne, 30 April 1911, pp. 5–6). The observations of the Member for Lang, Sir William Johnson, about the early survey camp and the plains come from his unpublished writings about Canberra held in the NLA (MS 216), while the Jimmy Catts quote was originally published in the *Canberra and District Historical Society Newsletter* (no. 422, April, May, 2009, p. 11).

Percy Schaeffe's quote about having to 'crawl on all fours ...' first appeared in *The Sydney Morning Herald* on 9 May 1927, while Arthur Perceval's description of Miller came from *Canberra's Foundations, 1911–1916*, reproduced in the *Canberra and District Historical Society Newsletter* (no. 426, December 2009/January 2010, p. 7).

O'Malley's 'Quaker, Shaker' quote comes from Hoyle (p. 117), while I sourced Mahony Griffin's 'For the love of Mike . . .' quote to Vernon, p. 13. The telegrams to and from Griffin regarding the competition, I've sourced to McGregor.

In late 2011 I interviewed Ian Batterham at the National Archives of Australia office at Mitchell. Thanks Ian, for patiently running through the complicated story of the Mahony Griffin drawings and the 'missing' one. My interview with Ian and his article ('The Walter Burley Griffin Design Drawings of the City of Canberra') in *Restaurator* (2009), informed the passages about the restoration of the pictures.

I extend my special thanks to Frank Moorhouse for his support, not least by granting me permission to quote extensively from the third of his 'Edith Trilogy' novels, *Cold Light* (Vintage, Sydney, 2011). The experiences of his protagonist Edith Campbell Berry in early Canberra – especially regarding the Mahony Griffin drawings, Causeway Hall and the lake – are a most welcome addition to these pages.

Thank you Friedhelm (Karl) Fischer for helping me to understand Griffin's casino, the 'pleasance' and of course his beer gardens (several would have been nice!). But as Hoyle (p. 117) pointed out, O'Malley wanted only a temperance hotel.

I found an original copy of George Taylor's *Building* magazine article in the 'Papers of Eric Nicholls relating to Walter Burley Griffin and Marion Mahony Griffin' (NLA, MS 9951/Box1), along with a plethora of other material relating to the Griffins, including Griffin's original speech to the Minneapolis Builders' Exchange where he described his plan as 'an expression of the democratic civic ideal', and the 1928 speech that follows.

The Dorothy Adams memoir is in the National Library (MS 8769).

Continuing City

The story of the provisional Parliament House was drawn from a number of the books already mentioned and also from Gay Hogan's *Parliament House, Canberra, 1927: Records Relating to the Design, Construction and Opening of the Provisional*

Parliament House (National Archives of Australia, Canberra, 1997), especially pp. 13 and 74.

Recollections by Charlie Law and 'one old resident' are among many stories collected by Ann Gugler, whose exhaustive research into the workers' camps – especially at Westlake – appears in her book *True Tales from Canberra's Vanished Suburbs of Westlake, Westridge and Acton* (A. Gugler, Canberra, 1999). Thanks Ann. I have also drawn on my previous independent research for my article 'Anzac: Endurance, Truth, Courage and Mythology' (*Meanjin*, spring, 2010).

Walter Sheen's written recollections are held by the National Library of Australia (MS 3908). The novelist Roger McDonald shared his Canberra stories with me during a long interview at his property outside Braidwood in spring 2011.

My newspaper column was published in the *Sunday Canberra Times* and the Sydney *Sun-Herald* on 21 August 2011.

Thank you Libby Stewart for dispelling the myth about the pies and sausage rolls (and for guidance on other primary resources) in an interview at Parliament House in late October 2011.

My account of the accidental death of Flying Officer Ewen comes from the daily newspaper reports (*The Age*, *The Sydney Morning Herald*, *The Argus*, *The Canberra Times*) in the days that followed, and also from the newspaper accounts of the subsequent coroner's inquiry.

Historian Lenore Coltheart gave me an extensive tour of Albert Hall while sharing her thoughts about the building's symbolism and neglect (surely the Commonwealth should fund its renovation for the Centenary). For the history of Albert Hall I relied on a series of papers by Lenore published in the *Canberra Historical Journal* (May 2011, May 2010 and August 2008). Lenore told me the story of *Bellona*, which I followed up using a number of sources including relevant newspaper reports (thanks Dave Reid) on *Dave's ACT* (www.davesact.com).

Canberra, by Kenneth Slessor, was published by Rigby, Adelaide, in 1966. Frank Hurley's *Canberra: A Camera Study*, was published by John Sands, Sydney, in 1961.

For information on Hugo Throssell, his suicide and his pistol, go to the Australian War Memorial website at cas.awm.gov.au/item/REL/11836.

The quotes from Michael McKernan (who became a great Brumbies supporter, even writing the team's history!) came from our interview on 31 October 2011.

Canberra writer and historian Jenny Horsfield has been a great supporter of this book. I am indebted to her for showing me around Tuggeranong homestead and telling me its story. For background about the early families of Tuggeranong and Lanyon, I referred to her book *Mary Cunningham: An Australian Life* (Ginninderra Press, Canberra, 2004).

I have quoted from the second edition of Donald Horne's *The Lucky Country* (Angus & Robertson, Sydney, 1965, p. 166), and I interviewed Aldo Giurgola at his apartment in March 2012.

Thank you Brett Odgers of the Canberra Burley Griffin Society, who went out of his way repeatedly to help me answer questions about the Griffins' Canberra years, their plan and the political compromises that befell it.

Thanks to Manlio and the Pancino family for permission to quote from Manlio's memoir. And thanks also to my dear friend Michael Brissenden and his family – especially Rosemary – for permission to quote from Bob's manuscripts held by the National Library of Australia (MS 8162).

I thank Lyn Mills for sharing her insights during an interview at Manuka on 9 November 2011. I also interviewed Alan Gould (15 December 2011), Jon Stanhope (25 November 2011) and Heather Henderson (31 January 2012) in their homes. I thank them all.

I thank Blanche d'Alpuget and Marion Halligan for sharing their reflections and observations. I quoted Blanche based on our discussion by Skype on 7 January 2012 (and subsequent email exchanges), and Marion after we talked at her home on 15 February 2012. I interviewed Robyn Archer in Canberra on 6 January 2012.

I had a long discussion with the ever-compelling and entertaining Jack Waterford on 1 November 2011, from which his quotes in the book are drawn. I also borrowed extensively from Jack's substantial library of Canberra books, pamphlets and ephemera. Thanks Jack.

Among the many other books that provided valuable insights were *Canberra 1912: Plans and Planners of the Australian Capital Competition*, by John Reps (Melbourne University Press, Carlton, 1997); *The Early Canberra House* (Federal Capital Press, Fyshwick, 1996); *Growing Up in Early Canberra*, by W.M. Rolland (Kangaroo Press,

Kenthurst, 1988); *A Witness to History: The Life and Times of Robert Broinowski*, by Richard Broinowski (Melbourne University Press, Carlton, 2001); *Canberra*, by Lionel Wigmore (Dalton Publishing, 1972); and *Developing Images: Mildenhall's Photographs of Early Canberra* (National Archives of Australia, Canberra, 2000).

I have sought, where relevant, to obtain copyright permission. Where this has not been possible, I welcome further information.

Thanks also to: Louise Adler, Foong Ling Kong, Peter Fray, Mike Bowers, Chris Hammer, Mark Dapin, Robyn Archer, Alex Sloane, Paul Cleary, Dennis Grant, Mike Pickering, Gia Metherell (for helping me find people), Mary Cunnane, Tony Wright, Bryan Dawe, Jeremy Thompson, Phil Dorling, Melanie Sim and the staff at the NLA's Petherick and Manuscript reading rooms.

Thank you John Mapps for editing my manuscript with such skill and sensitivity. Any remaining errors are mine. Thanks to Josephine Pajor-Markus for her design of this book, and to David Atkinson for the map.

This book would have been impossible without the support and love of Lenore Taylor, who ensures that family life continues while I write.

Finally I would like to thank Kathy Bail and Phillipa McGuinness for inviting me to contribute to the eminent City Series with *Canberra*. The company is illustrious.